D1274759

The
Friendship
Book

A THOUGHT FOR
EACH DAY IN 2013

"Oh give me the hour that I love best
When the heart is quite warm and the words are free,
When I sit at ease and converse with a friend,
Who sits at ease and converses with me."

George Crabbe (1754-1832)

January

AT the beginning of another New Year, the Lady of the House and I wish you the best of New Years, peace of mind and spirit, good health and many friends. May you find in the words of the Devonshire poet Samuel Taylor Coleridge:
"... *All seasons shall be sweet to thee,*
Whether the Summer clothe the general earth with
greenness,
or the redbreast sit and sing
Betwixt the tufts of snow on the bare branch
of mossy apple-tree."
A Happy New Year to you all!

WHEN the great explorer Ernest Shackleton sailed to Antarctica his plan to trek to the South Pole went awry when his ship became trapped in the crushing ice.

He and his crew were forced to abandon ship and an epic rescue operation began. I was surprised to read, however, that amongst the supplies Shackleton took from the sinking ship was a crewman's banjo! Whatever hardships his men were about to face, he knew they would be stronger with the sound of music to lighten their hearts.

Thankfully, we aren't trapped in the Antarctic, but some challenges and concerns in life can indeed be serious. Our words, offered in kindness, can be the music that lifts a heart and makes the journey worth carrying on with.

Thursday — *January 3*

FRANK LAUBACH was a missionary who worked and lived in the Philippines among those who saw Christians as their enemies. Over the next few decades he converted many by his teaching and example.

On the first few pages of his 1930 diary he wrote: "To be able to look backwards and say, 'This, this, has been the finest year of my life,' that is glorious! But anticipation. To be able to look ahead and say, 'The next year can and shall be better,' that is more glorious!"

Let's take this advice and step into a new year, determined to look forward rather than back and determined to make each new month ever more glorious!

Friday — *January 4*

WHILE thumbing through a 19th-century book of poems I found these beautiful lines by Josephine Canning:
Like music heard on the still water,
Like pines when the wind passeth by,
Like pearls in the depth of the ocean,
Like stars that enamel the sky,
Like June and the odour of roses,
Like dew and the freshness of morn,
Like sunshine that kisses the clover,
Like tassels of silk on the corn,
Like notes of the thrush in the woodland,
Like brooks where the violets grow,
Like rainbows that arch the blue heavens,
Like clouds when the sun dippeth low,
Like dreams of Arcadian pleasures,
Like colours that gratefully blend,
Like everything breathing of pureness,
Like these, is the love of a friend.

Saturday — *January 5*

*STEP lightly through the coming year
Whatever it may bring,
Have courage in the Winter storms
And reach out to the Spring.
And catch the sunshine when you can,
It lifts the heart and mind,
Be cheerful in the darker days
Though life may seem unkind.*

*Step bravely when the road is steep
And climb the highest hill,
Then looking up towards the stars
Your hopes and dreams fulfil.
Still cherish faith, and love and joy,
Dispelling doubt and fear,
Tomorrow beckons, look ahead,
Step lightly through the year!*
                                        Iris Hesselden

Sunday — *January 6*

IN a recent poll to find the year's most inspiring person, homeless Detroit man Charles Moore came higher up the list than a businessman who had given what was, until then, the biggest charitable donation in history.

Penniless Moore found a substantial but not huge amount of cashable bonds in a bin and returned them to their rightful owner. Why did this touch people more than the incredibly generous gift of the business man? It was because Moore gave all he had.

"Jesus said, 'I tell you the truth, this poor widow has put more into the treasury than all the others. They gave out of their wealth; but she, out of her poverty, put in everything.'"
                                        (Mark 12:44)

Monday — *January 7*

AS the January sales begin and coach companies are offering trips to the latest super-sized shopping centres, may I share this tale about the philosopher Plato?

Keen to get the patronage of a "celebrity", some Greek entrepreneurs asked him to visit a particular marketplace. The market was huge and Plato spent hours wandering around. When he came out he was clearly amazed, and the waiting entrepreneurs were desperate to hear what he thought.

"Well," said Plato, "I never knew it was possible to buy so many things I will never need!"

Tuesday — *January 8*

A FRIEND of the Lady of the House was feeling a bit overwhelmed by problems.

"Are you buried or planted?" the Lady of the House asked her. And then, by way of explanation, she said: "If you're buried under your problems then there's nothing you can do, but if you're planted in them then they become the fertiliser that helps you grow."

Helen continued to look puzzled but something in her expression suggested to me that the Lady of the House had just planted a very useful idea.

Wednesday — *January 9*

ONE day we were discussing with our friend John how difficult it is to know what to do for the best sometimes when he grinned and said: "Follow your heart. It might be on the left – but it's always right!"

Just a little confusing but amazingly, simply, true at the same time!

Thursday — *January 10*

A COMEDY programme on television decided, just for one week, to introduce a "happiness gauge". It took the form of a digital pointer sweeping across a rainbow-shaped gauge. When a comedian cracked a joke and the audience applauded, the screen would come up and the viewers could see the pointer move. The further it moved, the more points the comedian got.

However, each time the audience saw the pointer appear they did a strange thing. They clapped even louder!

All this goes to show one thing. Making people happy – makes everyone happy.

Friday — *January 11*

THE old lilac tree in the garden had stood its ground for decades. It was well established when our old friend Mary moved into her home and, years later, it was still producing beautiful blooms every summer.

But one morning, after one of the worst storms in living memory, she discovered that its branches had been ripped off and the old tree had been split down the middle. Barely a stump remained. It would have been simple to plant something new in its place, but Mary decided to see what the future would bring.

This area of the garden looked bare and empty for some time, but at last green shoots began to rise from the stump and the leaves gradually became healthy and glossy.

The American author, Christian Nestell Bovee, faced many a setback in his life, but he learned to look forward, not back: "When all else is lost, the future still remains," he wrote.

Happily, the future looks bright for Mary's treasured lilac tree.

Saturday — *January 12*

JENNY was reminiscing about her father who had died more than a decade ago. "I think about him most days," she told the Lady of the House. Then, a little wistfully, she added: "Sometimes it's with my mind but sometimes it's just with my heart."

Just? I'm sure there's no "just" about it. In fact, I can't think of a way I would rather be thought of. What better way to keep someone in mind, than to keep them in your heart?

Sunday — *January 13*

SOME birds can reach great heights by riding on thermals, updrafts of warm air, but the bird that flies the highest doesn't use them. The eagle spreads its wings and reaches the greatest heights by rising on the winds that bring storms. While all kinds of chaos breaks loose down below the eagle just rises above it.

Remember it's not the troubles in life that dictate whether we fall or rise, it's how we handle them. And with faith we have the ultimate "updraft".

"And this is the will of him who sent me, that I shall lose none of all that he has given me, but raise them up at the last day." (John 6:39)

Monday — *January 14*

THE Lady of the House nodded in agreement when she read these words in a magazine one day:
"A mind is like a parachute,
I heard it once proposed.
It's wonderful when open –
But not much good when closed!"

Tuesday — *January 15*

"CIRCUMSTANCES may appear to wreck our lives and God's plans, but God is not helpless among the ruins. Our broken lives are not lost and useless. God takes our calamity and uses it victoriously, working out His wonderful plan of love."

After he wrote these words Eric Liddell, the Scottish missionary, was imprisoned by the Japanese army. In the camp he suffered from a brain tumour and died without seeing again the family he had sent to safety. Surely his life had been wrecked.

But I heard that his Chinese students, although very senior in years, still follow his example and preach in his memory. The good they've done and the lives they have changed over the past 60 years could be compared to a flock of phoenix rising from the ashes of Liddell's life.

Never despair. When things seem bleak, remember that you are still part of a "wonderful plan of love".

Wednesday — *January 16*

STILLNESS is a doorway,
A space within the mind,
A place we may abide in
And leave the world behind,
A realm of tender silence,
Of nurturing and calm,
Where hopefulness and healing
Enfold us in their balm.
It waits for you to find it,
Just let life's hustle cease
And enter through that doorway
To wisdom, and to peace.
Margaret Ingall

Thursday — *January 17*

AS well as being a legend of the silver screen and generally being considered one of the world's most beautiful women, Sophia Loren is also a mother, grandmother – and a cook!

Her secret for keeping folk well fed could be applied with equal success to almost anything to do with families or friends. "The most indispensable ingredient of all home cooking," she once said, "is love for those you are cooking for."

Friday — *January 18*

DEEP streams usually run smoothly and quietly. They have the same rocks and obstacles to overcome as their noisy, shallow counterparts, but they are so full that they can rise above those difficulties so a casual observer would never know they were there.

Whether our lives are turbulent and noisy, or smooth and graceful doesn't depend on how many or how few problems they contain. It depends on how full they are.

Saturday — *January 19*

THE great Russian writer, Dostoevsky, had a deep and lifelong love of wildlife. He once expressed his feelings this way:

"Love all animals. God has given them the rudiments of thought and joy. Don't trouble them, don't harass them, don't deprive them of their happiness, don't work against God's will."

His words are as timely today as they were when he wrote them.

Sunday — **January 20**

AFTER summers spent gathering what wealth they could, some Native American tribes would hold a "potlatch" ceremony. The wealth of the tribe, or individuals, would be redistributed, or simply given away.

The more someone gave, the higher the esteem they would be held in. Sometimes individuals would give away all their possessions, but often they were rewarded up to the same amount at the next potlatch.

It might sound quite basic, but don't we have something similar? I'm thinking of the words in Luke 6:38:

"Give and it will be given to you: good measure, pressed down, shaken together and running over will be put into your bosom. For with the same measure that you use, it will be measured back to you."

Monday — **January 21**

MY friend Jim was reading that classic book on climbing, Edward Whymper's "Scrambles In The Alps", when he came on this advice to those who venture on to the high tops: "Do nothing in haste, look well to each step, and from the beginning think well what may be the end."

Yes, sound advice to climbers but not a bad code for all of us to follow, day by day and year by year.

Tuesday — **January 22**

SEAN, a good friend, shared with me this proverb: "All the flowers of all the tomorrows are in the seeds of today."

This is an excellent way to remember that nothing – not even if it's as tiny as a seed – should ever be dismissed as being too unimportant to bother with.

Wednesday – *January 23*

AFTER a fire ravaged parts of Chicago, the evangelist D. L. Moody went to New York to raise money for the victims. One wealthy businessman donated a large amount and encouraged his friends and colleagues to help out as well.

On leaving, Moody thanked the man and urged him to visit Chicago where he might in some small way repay the favour. The reply was: "Don't wait for me, Mr Moody. Do it to the first fellow who comes along."

A businessman he definitely was, but he could surely lay equal claim to being a Samaritan – and a Good one at that.

Thursday – *January 24*

HENRY was with a few friends when everyone began to discuss the unsettled weather they had been experiencing. They all complained about it except Jack, who at last broke his silence.

"Well," he said in his usual quiet way, "this is how I look at it. If we don't have a winter, there will be no spring, and if there is no spring we can't have a summer or an autumn. We need all the seasons."

And of course, he was right, wasn't he? Think of it that way and wintry weather perhaps doesn't seem so bad after all.

Friday – *January 25*

IN the 14th century the Persian poet Hafiz of Shiraz wrote: "Even after all this time the sun never says to the earth, 'You owe Me.' Look what happens with a love like that. It lights the whole sky."

If the earth owes a big Thank You to the sun, how much more do we who live on that beautiful planet owe the One who made the sun?

Saturday — *January 26*

AN interviewer asked rock guitarist Buddy Miller about his riff on a Robert Plant song. "That bit just jumps out of the speakers," the interviewer said. "How did you do that?"

"Trying to do something better," Miller laughed.

There's an old saying that you should aim for the stars because even if you don't get there, you might still reach the moon. Like Buddy Miller you may amaze yourself, and others, by the wonderful things you achieve on the way to doing "something better."

Sunday — *January 27*

IN the classic children's story, "Alice In Wonderland", Alice comes to a fork in the road. "Cheshire-puss," she asks the cat in the tree. "Would you tell me please, which way I ought to go from here?"

"That depends a good deal on where you want to go," the cat replies. When Alice confesses she doesn't much care where she's going, the cat replies that, if that's the case, it doesn't much matter which way she goes.

Knowing where you're going is the important thing, and those of us who choose Heaven as our destination will find the path already under our feet.

"Whether you turn to the right or to the left, your ears will hear a voice behind you saying, 'This is the way: walk in it'."

(Isaiah 30:21)

Monday — *January 28*

WHAT'S the happiest kind of life you could possibly have? It's a subject that's wide open for debate, but I'd like to suggest that this old adage has a sound perspective on the subject:

"Blessed is the person who is too busy to worry in the daytime – and too sleepy to worry at night!"

Tuesday — *January 29*

DO you believe that prayers are always answered? It's a huge question, and one which has prompted many deep discussions, brought forth many different opinions and revealed many different experiences.

Personally I like the words of S. H. B. Masterman who expressed the view that "God often comforts us, not by changing the circumstances of our lives, but by changing our attitude towards them."

In its own unique way, I think this is every bit as miraculous.

Wednesday — *January 30*

THE two young girls in the back of the car were bored. "Tell us a story, Dad," they begged, and after a few minutes thought, he began.

It was all about a colony of rabbits and Richard Adams' daughters loved the tale so much he later made it into a novel. Over a dozen publishers rejected the manuscript but when it appeared at last, it became a best seller, appealing both to adults and children.

"Watership Down" is now a classic, proving that a good tale well told will always win hearts and minds.

Thursday — *January 31*

FOR the Pre-Raphaelites the most important colour was the white base they painted on. For Pablo Picasso in his blue period the most important colour was, of course, blue, but Marc Chagall, the Russian-French artist had his own opinion on what was important.

"In our life," he wrote, "there is a single colour, as on an artist's palette, which provides the meaning of life and art — it is the colour of love."

Snowgirl

February

Friday — **February 1**

IS there anything about your daily routine that really irritates you? If so, I'm sure you're not alone!

It certainly annoyed postman Eric that whenever he tried to deliver letters to one house on his round, he had to make his way through a front garden that was rapidly turning into a jungle.

However, he also knew who lived in the property — an elderly man who was unable to tackle the job himself. After weeks of silent grumbling, Eric realised that there was one obvious solution; he could offer to do the job himself at no charge.

Although his suggestion was at first only rather grudgingly accepted, Eric happily began his self-appointed task and soon found it to be such a satisfying way of relaxing that he was volunteering to help more people on his round.

The result was one contented volunteer and even more grateful garden owners. And all this came from a little lateral thinking, so let's think about trying it, too, next time we have an attack of the grumbles!

Saturday — **February 2**

FAITH lights a lantern that burns ever long,
Faith lights a lantern that shines ever strong,
For though skies may darken and storm clouds may roll,
Still faith's flame glows steady to calm and console,
No matter how wind-tossed or battered or drenched,
The light of faith's lantern can never be quenched.

Margaret Ingall

Sunday — *February 3*

EVERY day Edward sweeps pavements, rakes leaves and gathers litter on the streets of his town. He is almost blind, but he cheerfully "likes to take care of God's business", as he puts it.

Those who meet Edward are greatly encouraged; he has a good memory for names and voices and often replies quoting a favourite hymn or Bible quote. One of the streets he takes care of is called Church Street and some locals call him the Church Street Pastor!

Edward feels that his role extends beyond keeping streets clean. As an ambassador of goodwill and a bright light in his community, he takes his responsibilities seriously:

"Well done, good and faithful servant! You have been faithful with a few things; I will put you in charge of many things." (Matthew 25:23)

Monday — *February 4*

MAY the words of this native American song fill your day with gentle harmony:
It is lovely indeed, it is lovely indeed.
I, I am the spirit within the earth,
The feet of the earth are my feet,
The legs of the earth are my legs,
The bodily strength of the earth is my strength,
The thoughts of the earth are my thoughts,
The voice of the earth is my voice,
The feather of the earth is my feather.
All that belongs to the earth belongs to me,
All that surrounds the earth surrounds me,
I, I am the sacred words of the earth.
It is lovely indeed, it is lovely indeed.

Tuesday — *February 5*

WHEN Heather retired from her demanding full-time job in a busy retail centre, I was taken aback to hear she had immediately taken up work in a charity shop, this time in a voluntary capacity.

"Ah, but being able to work entirely for the love of it makes all the difference," she said when I expressed my surprise. "My old job paid the bills and so on, but this one pays me in friendship, laughter, interest and in knowing that what I do is absolutely worthwhile."

It was Winston Churchill who observed: "We make a living by what we get, but we make a life by what we give."

Wednesday — *February 6*

"FRIENDSHIP, on the other hand, serves a great host of different purposes all at the same time. In whatever direction you turn, it still remains yours. No barrier can shut it out. It can never be untimely; it can never be in the way. We need friendship all the time, just as much as we need the proverbial prime necessities of life, fire and water."

Wise words indeed. So can that be the latest wisdom from a highly qualified psychologist, or some experienced agony aunt? No, those were the words of Cicero who lived over 2000 years ago. Some things never change!

Thursday — *February 7*

WHETHER you've actually been asked for your opinion, or chosen to give it anyway, I can think of no better piece of advice than this from our old friend Anon:

"Speak softly and sweetly. If your words are soft and sweet they won't be so hard to swallow if you have to eat them."

Nor will you get indigestion!

Waiting Patiently

Friday — **February 8**

HAVE you ever heard of Rachel Carson? Perhaps not, despite the fact that her work has altered the quality of our world for the better. She is credited as being the mother of the green movement, one of the first people to bring to general notice just how carelessly we treat our environment.

Born in small-town America, she later studied English, then biology and zoology. Using her knowledge and her gift for writing, she penned a book called "Silent Spring" in 1962 in which she drew attention to the damage being done by pesticides. Though criticised at the time by the powerful voices of industry, the public took this book not just to its heart but to its mind.

Sadly, Rachel Carson died too early to see just how thriving the green movement has become, yet this book is still a lasting memorial to her achievements.

"She put the fire into the tinderbox of the environmental movement," Friends of the Earth said. And that is reason enough for us all to be grateful.

Saturday — **February 9**

ARCHBISHOP Desmond Tutu played a major part in the peaceful ending of apartheid in South Africa. He saw that revenge and recrimination could only hold his country back, and his daughter, Naomi, shared her father's forward-looking attitude.

"Most of the people who prepared the way for us," she wrote, "will not ask us to pay them back. What they do ask is that we make this world a better place for those who come after us."

Make the world a better place? How can we do that? Perhaps by following this example and replacing old grievances with a smile and a hand held out in friendship.

Sunday — *February 10*

SUNDAY school has been a regular and enjoyable part of life for many children. But who would have guessed that in its early days it provoked huge controversy?

In the 1790s the notion of literacy for the masses was viewed with considerable suspicion. If working-class youngsters were taught to read the Bible, what was to stop them going on to read more widely – and who knew where that might lead?

However, the attempt to suppress "dangerous" Sunday Schools failed, and they continued to thrive, becoming an uplifting social focus of many a small community.

So full marks to all the pioneering teachers who braved disapproval in order to enrich many young lives.

Monday — *February 11*

WHEN Pauline got her first parking ticket she was understandably upset. But instead of complaining she went and paid it straight away. She swallowed what she thought of as justifiable anger and instead went out of her way to help or simply smile at as many people as she could that day.

As Portuguese author Fernando Pessoa once wrote: "Stones in my way? I pick them all up. One day I will build a castle with them."

Tuesday — *February 12*

DO you want to make changes in your life, but are afraid that you may have left it too late? Then take courage from what American scientist Ralph Gerard has to say:

"No age or time of life, no position or circumstance, has a monopoly on success. Any age is the right age to start doing!"

Petal
Perfection

Wednesday – *February 13*

GETTING up from our cosy bed in the morning often doesn't appeal. On bright summer mornings we might leap from bed full of enthusiasm, but on an icy winter's morning it's altogether different.

Still, these words by an unknown writer might make it all a little easier. "Every morning is a challenge. Waking from sleep is like being born again. Leaving our bed and faring forth means that we have a new opportunity – an opportunity to do better than we have ever done before."

So leave that snooze button alone and rise to the challenges of the day ahead!

Thursday – *February 14*

ROY Rogers was the king of the Hollywood cowboys in a career that included over a hundred films. His horses, including the famous Trigger, shared his star treatment and enjoyed the best of care.

Rogers once said to one of the young men in his employment: "If you're going to look after my horses you better learn to ride." Then he gave some lessons and that new talent enabled the would-be actor to get into Westerns and make a name for himself.

"Mr Rogers was very kind to me," film legend Glenn Ford later recalled.

You never know where a good deed will end up!

Friday – *February 15*

I'D been grumbling about always seeming to be short of time, when the Lady of the House smilingly reminded me of these words from C. S. Lewis: "The future is something which everyone reaches at the rate of 60 minutes an hour, whatever he does, whoever he is."

Ah, well, perhaps I do have as much time as everybody else after all, come to think of it!

Saturday — **February 16**

SUSAN has a canary called Rosie, who is rarely to be found in her cage. Rosie loves the sun and will stretch out wherever she can find a warm, bright patch.

One afternoon Susan looked everywhere for Rosie; she began to worry until she finally found her basking between the tea cups in the china cabinet where a sliver of sunshine could be seen.

Rosie's cheerful pursuit of sunlight reminds me of Max Lucado's book "Cure For The Common Life: Living In Your Sweet Spot." He writes that there is a cure for the doldrums of daily life — the answer is to find your sweet spot. God tailored your life to fit an empty space in His jigsaw puzzle and once you find your spot, life makes sense, he argues.

Each one of us is created to fill a unique place on earth in a special way. Keep this in mind and you'll be able to do all things with courage and confidence.

Sunday — **February 17**

THE oldest man-made structure in California's Yosemite National Park is an elegant non-denominational wooden chapel. It's a favourite location for weddings and welcomes many visitors.

When admiring its simple beauty you might notice something a little unusual for a church. There's no stained glass to be seen and all of the windows are plain glass.

It's only when you stand inside and look out towards the wonders of Yosemite that you see why. The best work of the most skilled craftsmen could not compare with the natural breathtaking grandeur of Yosemite!

"God saw all that he had made, and it was very good. And there was evening and there was morning – the sixth day."

(Genesis 1:31)

Monday — **February 18**

TO be born with a cleft palate in 1880 was a misfortune that didn't lead for an easy life and, as a result, young Reginald Farrer's childhood was a solitary one, interrupted by operations to correct his condition.

His free time was spent exploring the limestone hills near his home in North Yorkshire, so perhaps it was only natural that he should embark upon a career as a plant collector, travelling the world to write home with joyful enthusiasm about all the new species he observed. When he returned he brought specimens with him, working hard to popularise alpine plants and rock gardens.

Sadly, he died aged 40 while travelling in Burma, but next time you pause to admire the delicate beauty of a rock plant, remember Reginald Farrer whose endeavours enriched our gardens and whose own early difficulties never blunted his sense of wonder.

Tuesday — **February 19**

DAWN is a life coach who has been through some extremely difficult times. She was widowed when young and brought up four children alone.

Her clients are drawn to her generous spirit and strength. She often weaves examples of her own struggles and successes into counselling sessions, giving those who come to see her a new perspective.

On Dawn's wall hangs a plaque with this quote by Shakti Gawain, inspirational author and teacher:

"We avoid the things that we're afraid of because we think there will be dire consequences if we confront them. But the truly dire consequences in our lives come from avoiding things that we need to learn about or discover."

Wise words for us to think about as we continue our journey through life.

Wednesday — **February 20**

JO had been using her new computer to do research for a dissertation, so I was interested to hear how she'd been getting on.

"All right," she replied cautiously, "but although the Internet can be a wonderful way of finding out things, it's not always as simple as you think — last night I accidentally pulled out one of the connecting wires from my laptop which meant I had to start all over again as I hadn't saved what I'd done."

Happily, I was able to console her with a quote from Emily Hilburn Sell about another kind of network: "Love is a force that connects us to every strand of the universe, an unconditional state that characterises human nature, a form of knowledge that is always there for us if only we can open ourselves to it."

And what's more, it doesn't rely on being plugged in!

Thursday — **February 21**

JANE has run the school orchestra for many years now, and while enjoying the challenge, she sometimes wonders how much good she actually achieves.

One day, I found her looking extremely cheerful. "I'm over the moon, Francis," she confirmed. "Young Cathy came to see me yesterday, except she's no longer a schoolgirl — she is in her thirties, has children of her own. But she called round especially to tell me how much she'd enjoyed being a member of the orchestra, and how she still loved making music. It was so unexpected and rewarding!"

It's good when selfless people like Jane realise just how valuable their efforts are. And if you haven't been told yet, remember the words of Edwin Hubbel Chapin: "Every action in our lives touches on some chord that will vibrate in eternity."

Building Sight

*Friday — **February 22***

*D*ON'T be afraid for you will be lifted,
Always have courage, facing each day,
Don't ever doubt, your faith will sustain you,
Hope is the lantern lighting your way.

Don't miss the sunshine, catch every glimmer,
Though skies are cloudy, look for a gleam,
Don't ever think you are forgotten,
Thoughts travel quickly, soft as a dream.

Don't be afraid, this life is for living,
Grasp every moment, whatever it brings,
Feel yourself lifted, high above trouble,
Carried aloft on an angel's wings.

Iris Hesselden

*Saturday — **February 23***

RATHER than walk along the pavement beside the busy main road every day, Pam longed to stroll through the woods on the other side of town.

The sound of birdsong had to be preferable to the noise of traffic, she reasoned, but the thought of a detour and an unknown route put her off. Her shoes would get wet and perhaps her clothes would get caught on thorns.

And so they did – the first few times she made the decision to change her route. Months later, Pam has a well-worn path to follow.

It's the same with life. We can follow the crowd, or do the thing that makes our soul sing. And in doing so, we make it easier for the next person who comes along our way.

I suppose Ralph Waldo Emerson meant the same when he wrote: "Do not go where the path may lead, go instead where there is no path, and leave a trail."

Sunday — *February 24*

AT the beginning of a church service, our old friend Mary's clergyman was looking solemn.

"Welcome," he said, "to the second Sunday in Lent. For all of you who have given up something at this time, well done! If you aren't allowing yourself to eat chocolate, that seems a good choice.

"But one thing for you to keep in mind," he went on, smiling, "is that there are Jaffa cakes to enjoy with coffee after the service today. So, if you are being strict with yourself when it comes to treats this Lent, you are allowed to go and peek at them and feel very self-righteous!"

Monday — *February 25*

DO as you would be done by
Is wise advice indeed,
For if we're kind and thoughtful
And help our friends in need,
Not only are we acting
The very way we should,
There is another bonus -
It makes us too feel good!
                M. J. Brison

Tuesday — *February 26*

SOMETIMES we don't get ahead in life because … Well, we just don't believe we can. But Alan Alda, star of the television series "M.A.S.H" and writer and director, had this to say about our expectations of ourselves:

"Begin challenging your own assumptions. Your assumptions are the windows on your world. Scrub them off every once in a while, and let the light in!"

Wednesday — **February 27**

FOR more than 10 years a small group of men and women dreamed of establishing the first Christian radio station in Kitchener-Waterloo, Ontario. It was an ambitious undertaking and not without challenges. Several people said it couldn't be done; one broadcaster voiced this opinion when he found out the station would be only 50 watts: "Go big, or go home."

But the group carried on, and Faith FM 94.3 was given its broadcasting licence. This little radio station began to send out God's message of love and hope over the airwaves 24 hours a day.

Faith FM's audience became both loyal and growing, ratings were excellent and plans were soon under way to increase the station's power. Listeners from around the world were able to pick up the signal on the Internet.

Faith FM 94.3 is a testament to vision and perseverance.

Thursday — **February 28**

WHEN David failed to gain acceptance to the university of his choice, his first reaction was to sulk. "I was too impatient to re-sit my exams," he said. "But I needed money, so I took the first job offered to me — as a general dogsbody in a small engineering factory."

But gradually, and almost despite himself, David became interested in his work. Eventually he started his own firm, and is now in charge of a loyal and hardworking team of workers.

"Best of all, it has given me the chance to pass on my own good luck, and to encourage young folk who come to work for me," he remarked.

It was John Ruskin who said: "The highest reward for a person's toil is not what they get for it, but what they become of it." If anyone should doubt that, think of David.

March

FIFTEEN-YEAR-OLD Thomas went on a mission-trip to volunteer among the many street people in the city of Philadelphia. He went with a team of teenagers and stayed for a week.

Thomas had begun the journey with some misgivings; it was a new and often intimidating experience for him, but later he came home rejuvenated and excited. Not only was he more thankful for what life had given him, he also said that he would never look at a homeless person or someone in need the same way again.

"It's easy to judge people without knowing a thing about them and to think they're all the same. I believe it's a mistake many of us make, but I know the thoughts I had towards the homeless left me as soon as I met them on the first day," Thomas explained.

A Haitian proverb says: "The rocks in the water don't know the misery of the rocks in the sun." In other words, we cannot understand another man or woman unless we walk in his or her shoes.

Today, if you meet someone with a need, consider how you might help to fill it.

IF, like our old friend Mary, you're getting a bit tired of the wind and the rain this time of year often brings, then look forward to the summer with these words from the second century written by Bishop Alexander:

"It takes God's weather to bring up God's flowers."

Sunday — **March 3**

FRIENDS of ours have a three-year-old daughter. She is cute as a button and her name is Eden. Did they call her that because they thought she was an angel? Was it because they were in paradise when she was born?

"No," they said. "It's because we know there will be good and bad in her, but she will always be a gift from God!"

"There are different kinds of gifts, but the same Spirit distributes them." (Corinthians 1 12:4)

Monday — **March 4**

IT'S lovely to go away on holiday but, if you are like the Lady of the House, you are perhaps not altogether sorry when the time comes to go home again. This verse, quoted to me many years ago, says a great deal:

We wander east,
We wander west,
We roam the world wide,
But the sweetest corner
And the best
Is just our own fireside.

Tuesday — **March 5**

OUR friend Jean is well known for her ability to get things done, no matter how challenging the situation. She was once asked the secret of her success and she replied:

"Well, I like to do things now, today, for one simple reason. You see, experience has taught me that tomorrow is often the busiest day of the week."

A thought worth jotting down in everyone's diary, surely!

Wednesday — *March 6*

DOES it sometimes seem to you that people believe a little less in the finer, nobler aspects of living? In the struggle to make a living, are some people forgetting how to live with a sense of style?

Vincent Van Gogh said: "In the end we shall have had enough of cynicism and scepticism and humbug and we shall want to live more musically."

In response to the artistic genius of Van Gogh let's add a little colour, a little dash and style to our lives. Let's do our little bit to make the world a more musical place!

Thursday — *March 7*

ONE day the Lady of the House received a card from her friend Enid, featuring a wonderful poem by Annie Johnson Flint. It inspired me so much that I'd like to share it here with you today.

God hath not promised
Skies always blue,
Flower-strewn pathways
All our lives through;
God hath not promised
Sun without rain,
Joy without sorrow,
Peace without pain.

But God hath promised
Strength for the day,
Rest for the labour,
Light for the way,
Grace for the trials,
Help from above,
Unfailing sympathy,
Undying love.

Friday — *March 8*

THE manager of the convalescent home was beaming all over as she told our old friend Mary: "A greetings card arrived this morning addressed to *The Lady in the End Room*."

She explained: "The elderly lady in that room has no relations or friends living nearby and she receives very little mail. A visitor must have heard about that and decided to send her such a lovely card. It's the nicest thing that has happened in a long time."

A small act of kindness, but just imagine what it must have meant to one lonely heart.

Saturday — *March 9*

I'D like to pass on to you today these little-known words of wisdom as spoken by Abraham Lincoln, President of the United States from 1861 to 1865:

"You do have to do your own growing no matter how tall your grandfather was."

Sunday — *March 10*

AT various times in history John, in its many different versions, has been the most popular name in the world. In different languages it has been adapted as Jan, Johan, Eugene, Johannes, Xuan, Hans, Janos, Iain, Evan … to name a few.

Its popularity means it has sometimes come to be seen as a common name. What does it mean? "God is gracious."

Isn't it a wonderful thought that the Grace of God is so common?

"The Lord be with your spirit. Grace be with you all."

(Timothy II, 4:22)

Lost In Thought

Monday — *March 11*

AUTHOR Edith Wharton said that for her the two most beautiful words in the English language were "summer afternoon".

Yes, they have an attractive sound and evoke thoughts of warm, sunny days. But what about "spring morning"? And don't autumn and winter have their own beauties, too?

I wonder what, for you, are the two most beautiful words?

Tuesday — *March 12*

THERE are times in life when people may be unkind to you or do you a disservice and you may feel an urge to get even. I well remember a childhood phrase where in such situations we would say: "I'll get you back for that."

But as I have grown older and wiser, I have learned to try to rise above such things and these words of John E. Southard are wise ones to keep in mind:

"The only people with whom you should try to get even are those who have helped you."

Wednesday — *March 13*

IT'S wonderful the pleasure
That a window box can bring,
To gladden lonely hearts with all
The flowers of the spring.

Such fragrance and such beauty
Are a part of nature's ways,
Sent to add a little brightness
To the seasons of our days.
Elizabeth Gozney

Thursday — *March 14*

"I KNOW life is a journey," Ann said, "but I didn't imagine it would take me quite so far!"

She had been telling the Lady of the House of her intended move to a village in Africa, where her husband had been offered a job with a medical mission. It would be a huge change of lifestyle for both of them but, despite a few concerns, they were determined to face the challenge with resolve, knowing it was what they had chosen to do.

Some of us, of course, aren't lucky enough to have a choice, for difficult challenges can sometimes arrive on our doorsteps whether we want them to or not. At times like that, it's good to remember the words of André Gide who said: "Man cannot seek new oceans unless he has the courage to lose sight of the shore."

If you are facing a journey into the unknown, may your voyage be calm and your arrival a happy one.

Friday — *March 15*

"I'VE often heard that March comes in like a lion," mused our old friend Mary looking out at the sullen sky. "But this year it seems to be slinking in more like a wet dog."

The aptness of her words made me smile, and yet I rather liked, I realised, the fact that so many things in life don't conform to our expectations. For example, when we find that a nondescript plant has suddenly produced brilliant flowers or when an unremarkable journey reveals unexpected glimpses of beauty.

Of course, such surprises do not always fall into the category of pleasant, but even they can highlight the nice ones.

So, you see, the fact I like a little serendipity in life probably comes as no surprise at all!

Saturday — *March 16*

ACTRESS Audrey Hepburn had her own clear insight into life's desirable qualities. She once advised:

"For attractive lips, speak words of kindness. For lovely eyes, seek out the good in people. For a slim figure, share your food with the hungry. For poise, walk with the knowledge that you need never walk alone."

Something for us all to think about today.

Sunday — *March 17*

SOMETIMES certain people seem to have something the rest of us lack. In the case of Mother Teresa of Calcutta, she seemed to have a direct line to God. How else could she live the life of deprivation, service and unconditional love that she did?

Now it seems Mother Teresa often despaired, often felt cut off from God and often felt her prayers went unanswered. But she did His work anyway! Her doubts and fears show there was no special connection, she was as human as the rest, but the way she lived her life shows just how wonderful ordinary humans can be.

"To this end I will labour, struggling with all His energy, which so powerfully works within me."   (Colossians 1:29)

Monday — *March 18*

DURING an end-of-term quiz the teacher looked around his class and asked: "Who was Joan of Arc?"

Eight-year-old Tim thought for a moment and then replied: "Noah's wife."

As a Cuban proverb says: "Life is short but a smile is only a second's effort."

Delightful Daffodil

Tuesday — **March 19**

THERE'S a painting called Cuisine des Anges by Batolome Murillo which hangs in the Louvre. It depicts the kitchen of a convent, but all the chores are being done by angels. One is setting a table, another carrying water, yet another boiling a kettle. A little cherub plays at their feet.

I think the artist wanted to suggest that even menial work may be done in an uplifting way. And when I look at this masterpiece it reminds me that we are often closer to Heaven in a family kitchen than anywhere else on earth.

Wednesday — **March 20**

A DIFFICULT path, is the road to success,
Its perils and pitfalls we scarcely may guess.
It often holds hazards, obstructions and blocks,
With brambles to snag us, and toe-stubbing rocks,
But oh, if we try, and refuse to turn back,
And never give up on our own chosen track
I'm sure when at last we approach journey's end,
We'll think of that path as our teacher and friend.

Margaret Ingall

Thursday — **March 21**

MOST of us are paying something for the place we live in. It might be a big house or a small flat but there will usually be a mortgage or rent to pay. What then, should we pay for our larger accommodation, this beautiful, awe-inspiring world we live in?

Sir Wilfred Grenfell, who was awarded a knighthood for his work as a medical missionary, had the perfect answer. "The service we render others," he wrote, "is the rent we pay for our room on earth."

Friday — *March 22*

WHY should you choose to wear a smile today? Well, it will make you feel better, but apart from that consider these points.

The chances are you will never know the good your smile does to the people you love, the neighbours you have a passing acquaintance with, the folk you pass on the street, because you never really know what they are going through.

When deciding whether to wear that smile or not, remember these words from St Francis of Assisi: "A single sunbeam is enough to drive away many shadows."

Saturday — *March 23*

*I*S *it any wonder,*
  When the sun shines in the sky,
That blackbirds sing and young
Lambs bleat and fluffy clouds float by.

Is it any wonder,
When new born babies smile,
We revel in the miracle
Ne'er failing to beguile.

Is it any wonder,
When stars shine from afar,
That peace descends and draws
A veil on nature's repertoire.

Is it any wonder,
That as through life we plod,
We marvel at the splendour
Of such gifts bestowed by God.
                    Brian H. Gent

Breaking Bread

Sunday — *March 24*

OUR old friend Mary passed on to me these words, ascribed to Rossiter Worthington Raymond:

"Life is eternal, and love is immortal, and death is only a horizon; and a horizon is nothing save the limit of our sight."

May these words uplift and comfort you at this special time of year.

Monday — *March 25*

OUR friend Chad's house was destroyed in one of California's wild fires. He and his family were unscathed, but most of their belongings went up in smoke.

"Well, to look on the bright side," Chad said later, "I'd discovered termites in the woodwork not long before the fire and it would have cost a lot of money to have it treated. But this way I got rid of the critters for free!"

It's one of the most wonderful attributes of human beings that we can make just about anything seem better with courage and a sense of humour!

Tuesday — *March 26*

WHEN Bill, my farmer friend, put down his coffee mug I saw the words. He told me his wife, Isobel, had them stencilled there to save him saying them so often: "Lazy folk take the most pains."

I'd never thought of Bill as lazy, so I raised an enquiring eyebrow.

"Oh, I am!" he insisted. "Well, lazy enough not to want to do a job twice. So, I take pains to do it right first time."

The world could do with more of Bill's brand of laziness, don't you think?

Wednesday — *March 27*

HOW do you do the seemingly impossible? Well, try taking one step at a time and not giving up.

Every year people died trying to cross the upper Zambezi River. Crispin Baleri, a missionary living nearby, decided something had to be done about it. The river is a thousand foot wide at that point, Brother Crispin had no money, no materials and no experience, but he knew it had to be done.

Five years later, after studying bridge construction from scratch, begging discarded cables from mining companies and never giving up his quest, he opened the Chinyingi Suspension Bridge. Now many people walk across it every day in complete safety.

Next time you find yourself facing a seemingly insurmountable situation, ask yourself — is it really impossible, or would you rather bridge the Zambezi?

Thursday — *March 28*

IT'S Maundy Thursday, the Thursday before Easter, the day when, by tradition, the monarch of Great Britain gives purses of specially minted coins to a select number of senior citizens, one man and one woman for each year of the sovereign's reign.

Did you know that the word "maundy" comes from the word "mandate" meaning a command? For the Maundy Ceremony is not just a quaint historical custom, but an acknowledgement of the instruction given by Christ at the Last Supper: "And now I give you a new commandment: love one another. As I have loved you, so you must love one another." (John 15:12)

At this time of year, let us all renew our commitment to these words and make them a real part of our lives, not just at Eastertide — but always.

Friday — *March 29*

NOT everyone has an easy time believing in the essential goodness of our world. Jessie Owens, the famous 20th-century Olympic athlete, had this advice about the goodness to be found around us: "It's all around you," he said. "Find it. Showcase it. And you'll start to believe it!"

As for the rest of us, we can do something similar. We can find it, showcase it – and prove it to be real!

Saturday — *March 30*

FRIENDS who have been separated for a long time usually find an amazing thing happens when they get back together – it's as if they have never been apart! This feeling is perfectly summed up in these words by an unknown author:

"Good friends are like the hands of a clock. They may only get to meet up every once in a while – but they are always connected!"

Sunday — *March 31*

THERE is a museum in Croatia dedicated to broken hearts – it is full of love letters and gifts from romances that didn't last. When I heard about this, at first I wondered if failed romances should be remembered like this.

Well, maybe, I reasoned after a while. After all, the relationships that work out and bring so much happiness wouldn't be half as challenging without the possibility of failure; the dawn sky wouldn't be as breathtaking without the dark of the night to compare it against; and without the heartbreak of Jesus on the cross, everlasting life would merely be an empty promise.

"Martha answered, 'I know he will rise again in the resurrection at the last day.'" (John 11:24)

April

THANK you, Lord, for the gift of spring,
The beauty all around,
The waking earth, the hope renewed,
Each joyful sight and sound.
Thank you for the help and healing
Through the winter time,
For comfort in the darkest days,
You helped our spirits climb.

Thank you for the longer days
The sunshine and the showers,
For all we share with those we love
Through many precious hours.
Be with us through the coming months
Whatever they may bring,
And help us walk a safer path,
And thank you, Lord, for spring.

Iris Hesselden

OUR old friend Mary came across these words in a book which the Lady of the House bought at a jumble sale:
"Life isn't about waiting for the storm to pass, it's about learning to dance in the rain."

A thought worth putting into practice when we hit a stormy stretch on life's road.

Wednesday — **April 3**

PATRICK looks after a famous garden which attracts thousands of visitors every year. Unlike many head gardeners, he did not attend college and had no formal training. His teachers, he says, were the plants themselves.

"I learned about azaleas from azaleas," he told me one day with a smile. "And about roses from my roses. I'm still learning from them every day."

We often forget that all knowledge is not stored in books but can be found in the world around us.

Thursday — **April 4**

HAVE you ever heard of International Pillow Fight Day? On 4th April almost 100 enthusiastic participants show up in Waterloo Town Square in Ontario, Canada, to pummel each other with pillows and have a good laugh. This good-natured event begins with everyone taking aim with abandon as feathers fly and onlookers cheer.

This massive pillow fight is organised by Urban Playground, a public space movement that encourages free events for all ages around the world. The goal is to partially replace time-consuming passive experiences like watching television with active fun happenings.

Studies show that having fun is an important part of our daily wellbeing. I think we would all agree it's a good thing to get more light-hearted moments into each day!

Friday — **April 5**

I BELIEVE in the sun even when it is not shining.
I believe in love even when not feeling it.
I believe in God even when He is silent.
Anon

Saturday — *April 6*

MANY of the castles that house centuries-old tapestries also run craft classes that show the public how these intricate handicrafts were made. At one event which our friend Ellen attended, an 18th-century tapestry was displayed, picture side up, and then turned over by the speaker.

Ellen was amazed to see how many loose ends and broken threads there were. The picture had looked perfect from the other side!

"That's because the strong threads take the strain for the weaker ones," she was told. "And the unbroken ones hold the broken ones together."

Leaving the castle Ellen looked across the city lying below it to the horizon beyond. What a beautiful tapestry, she thought.

Sunday — *April 7*

SOME time ago, Hazel started turning down her friend Meg's invitations to pop round for tea. Meg, puzzled by this behaviour, was at first tempted to take it as a personal snub until her common sense prevailed, and she decided to drop in unannounced.

"I found Hazel sitting at home, quite upset," said Meg. "It was all to do with something trivial and she hadn't wished to burden me with the details. Luckily some advice from the Bible managed to persuade her otherwise, and we had a long chat which made us both feel better.

"We recalled the words from Proverbs 17:17: 'Friends always show their love. What are brothers for if not to share a trouble'?"

Thank goodness for friends like Meg who understand that whether we are brothers, sisters, friends or family — we are still all the children of God.

THE FRIENDSHIP BOOK

Monday — *April 8*

OUR friend John was pulling out weeds in his vegetable plot as I passed by one afternoon. "Oh, I don't mind the weeds," he said with a grin when I sympathised with him. "They give me something to fight against. Growing my vegetables would be too easy without them, you know.

"Whatever we do in life, there has to be a bit of a challenge and I like to think of it as a friendly feud. Sometimes they win but more often I do. It's all part of the game, isn't it?"

A good way to see the way ahead, surely, whenever there are obstacles in our way.

Tuesday — *April 9*

JOHN Richard Green was a 19th-century English historian. Even though he never reached old age he had a memorable appreciation of life summed up in these words:

"What seems to grow fairer to me as life goes by is the love, grace and tenderness of it; not its wit, cleverness and grandeur of knowledge … just the laughter of little children, and the friendship of friends, and cosy talks by the fireside, and the sight of flowers, and the sound of music."

Wednesday — *April 10*

FOR many years our old friend Mary's mother kept this framed quote on her writing desk. It now takes pride of place hanging over Mary's desk, reminding her each day of the power of our words:

Flatter me, and I may not believe you
Criticise me, and I may not like you
Ignore me, and I may not forgive you
Encourage me, and I may not forget you.
William Arthur Ward

Thursday — *April 11*

I WONDER how many readers have heard of Sir Harry Lauder. In his day, few people would not have recognised his name, for he was a famous Scottish music hall entertainer, much loved for his humour and his songs.

He did, however, know his share of hardship, suffering early poverty and later, like many others, undergoing the pain of losing his son in the Great War. He himself entertained the forces in both the First and Second World Wars, and it's said that one of his most famous songs, "Keep Right On To The End Of The Road", was written to encourage the troops. It includes these words:

Though you're tired and weary, still journey on
Till you come to your happy abode,
Where all the love you've been dreaming of
Will be there at the end of the road.

I hope Harry Lauder found what he was dreaming of, for he brought comfort and pleasure to so many.

Friday — *April 12*

"I SUPPOSE it's basic human nature to try to cling on to things," mused the Lady of the House as we watched a toddler refusing to be parted from a large muddy stick he'd picked up in the park. We smiled as, after much persuasion from his mother, he finally exchanged it for a jelly baby, but it did rather reinforce the truth of her observation.

Even as adults we tend to hang on to many things for which we have no need, in the mistaken belief that bestowing them on someone else would somehow make us vulnerable. Writer Maya Angelou believed that exactly the opposite was true: "I have found that among its other benefits, giving liberates the soul of the giver," she wrote.

And I think that's an even better exchange than a jelly baby!

Saturday — *April 13*

YORKSHIRE folk are noted for their good sense and their love of a bargain. One day my friend Tom, originally from Harrogate, said: "There's nothing I like better or enjoy more than a long walk against the wind on a dry day in spring – it makes a new man of me and it's cheap, too!"

Compared to the price of gym membership I would say that was indeed a bargain. And this spring, as usual, there's bound to be enough wind to go around!

Sunday — *April 14*

HAVE you heard the tale of the Cherokee boy's rite of passage? He was blindfolded and sat on a tree stump in the middle of the woods. His big test was to sit there all night until the sun rose in the morning.

The youngster was understandably scared, his imagination running wild. Every noise, he was convinced, must be a wild animal about to eat him alive! But his courage held. When the morning sun warmed his face the boy — now a man — whipped off his blindfold. The first thing he saw was his father who had sat silently by his side the whole night long.

If danger had threatened his father would have protected him, just like our Father will. "We live by faith, not by sight."

(Corinthians II 5:7)

Monday — *April 15*

I CAME across these words from the famous entertainer Bob Hope the other day. They only take a moment to read but don't they just hit the nail on the head?

"If you haven't any charity in your heart, you have the worst kind of heart trouble."

Tuesday — **April 16**

OUR friend Alan was 12 years old when he wrote in his school jotter about high white clouds, birds singing and gardens "like circuses" with all the different coloured flowers. He ended his essay with this:

"I saw a man ploughing and he waved his hand to me. I don't know him but I expect he just felt like doing that. People often do on a sunny morning in springtime. I was sorry when the school bell rang."

How wonderful if Alan – and all the rest of us – could discover that "springtime" feeling in our hearts, the emotion that makes us want to wave to strangers just for the sheer joy of the day.

Wednesday — **April 17**

APOLO Anton Ohno is an Olympic speed skater who also appeared on the television programme "Dancing with the Stars" in the United States. Asked about his drive to win, he said: "Winning does not always mean coming in first — real victory is in arriving at the finish line with no regrets because you know you've gone all out."

Now, we might never go "all out" as quickly as a speed skater, but we can cross the finishing line at the end of each day with the same sense of satisfaction after giving that day the very best we had to give.

Thursday — **April 18**

LIFE can be difficult at times, it is true, but it can also be overwhelmingly wonderful!

This is why I am grateful for this reminder which I read recently: "When life gives you a hundred reasons to cry, show it that you have a thousand reasons to smile."

THE FRIENDSHIP BOOK

Friday — *April 19*

KIP Keino was orphaned young and brought up by an aunt in a poor Kenyan village. What chance, you might ask, did he have of making a mark on the world?

But in the 1968 Olympics, Keino won the 1500 metres, despite having to jog a mile just to get to the stadium! A glittering running career followed but he remained a modest man who used his fame to build schools in his homeland and help thousands of orphans.

What motivated such inspirational kindness? Keino said: "I came into this world with nothing. I will leave with nothing. While I am here I will be mindful of those people who need my help."

Saturday — *April 20*

A SUBTLE fragrance fills the air
And drifts among the trees,
As blossoms on the laden boughs
Are shaken by the breeze.

When sunbeams dance upon the blooms
All bathed in golden light,
The fragile petals brushed with dew
Seem frail and fairylike.

The trees are dressed in springtime's best
Arrayed in bridal lace,
For nature's hand has deftly worked
With artistry and grace.

On branch adorned with frothy spray
A thrush begins to sing,
Acknowledging in melody
The splendour of the spring.

Kathleen Gillum

Sunday — *April 21*

DURING an evening service, Jane heard the clergyman talk of Doubting Thomas when Jesus said to him: "Because you have seen me you have believed. Blessed are those who have not seen and yet have believed . . ."

The clergyman then began to define belief. "Faith is kind of hard to explain," he said, "but perhaps it could be compared to something like a bird singing in the darkness because it knows morning is coming."

Jane then thought of something that John Calvin, the French-born theologian, had said: "For the little singing birds sang of God, the animals acclaimed him, the elements feared and the mountains resounded with him, the rivers and springs threw glances towards him, the grasses and the flowers smiled."

Monday — *April 22*

SIR John Lubbock was a banker, philanthropist, politician and botanist. "Punch" magazine once published a cartoon of him as a "busy bee". Tiring as his daily round must have been, he knew there were worse things for the soul.

"A day of worry," he wrote, "is more exhausting than a day of work."

So, let's not go down that road. The next time you find yourself beset by worries be a busy bee. Put yourself to work, for someone else's sake – and for yours!

Tuesday — *April 23*

WHEN "God gives us a rocky road to travel, he ensures that we have sturdy boots for the journey." These comforting words, sent to me by a Welsh reader, are inspirational when our days are troubled and life is uncertain.

Wednesday — *April 24*

BARBARA is one of those people we could almost take for granted. Have you a letter to post? Well, she'll do it on her way to the shops. Do you need a cake-maker or a tea-pourer for the village fête? Barbara will volunteer.

"You see, before I retired," she explained, "I was so busy at work that I begrudged giving extra time to anyone, and even after I'd stopped working I continued to think that way.

"Then I suddenly realised that on the few occasions I did offer help to someone, I always found it really rewarding. Nowadays you might call it my most enjoyable hobby!"

What a perfect demonstration of those words from Piero Ferrucci: "It's all really, very simple. You don't have to choose between being kind to yourself and others. It's one and the same."

Thursday — *April 25*

WHEN you are already the busy mother of eight children, anyone might be excused the extra chore of becoming a prison visitor — particularly when the year is 1813 and society does not encourage any woman to venture beyond her domestic role.

However, committed Quaker Elizabeth Fry was too concerned about the appalling conditions of the inmates of Newgate to abandon her cause, and it's thanks to her inspirational efforts that many prison reforms came into being.

Happily, Elizabeth Fry's story did not go unrecorded, and I was reminded of it again when I read these words from Norman B. Rice: "Dare to reach out your hand into the darkness, to pull another hand into the light."

May we all have the courage to help make the world a more enlightened place.

Friday — *April 26*

SIR Winston Churchill, who led his country in many difficult times, once gave this sound advice for anyone facing a problem, big or small:

"A pessimist sees the difficulty in every opportunity but an optimist does better – he sees the opportunity in every difficulty."

Neatly put, isn't it?

Saturday — *April 27*

FILM star Kiefer Sutherland could easily be forgiven for hesitating when asked where he's from. He was born in England, raised in Canada and has spent a large part of his life working in the United States.

But there is no uncertainty, no hesitation when it comes to his personal philosophy. It's a simple idea he inherited from his grandfather and one the world might benefit from adopting: "Never walk past a man in the street when he's down."

Sunday — *April 28*

A YOUNG evangelist was setting up a board at the entrance to the shopping centre. On it he wrote: "If God exists – why do people suffer?" As I walked away, I wondered about the question and how's this for the answer that came to mind almost at once?

Do you think, if they could feel, roses would enjoy being pruned back? Do you think they relish having all that manure dumped on them? I mused. Well, no, but what is the end result? Better roses, of course!

"So be truly glad. There is wonderful joy ahead, even though you have to endure many trials for a little while."

(Peter 1 1:6)

Monday — *April 29*

THERE'S a true story told of twin girls who were born prematurely. Because they had been born so early they were put into separate incubators, but almost immediately the smaller baby began to fail. The doctors did all they could, but nothing seemed to help.

Then a nurse decided to do something different. She brought the weak baby to the stronger one. As she laid them together, the stronger baby reached out, with her eyes still closed, and put her arm over her sister's shoulder. From then on, the weaker baby started to recover and today both are healthy young women thoroughly enjoying life.

Now if a newborn child can do that, think what you, with a hug, a handshake or a pat on the back, can do for someone else who may be feeling as isolated as that small baby who might not have made it — but did!

Tuesday — *April 30*

"I'VE been visiting my aunt," Monica said. "She lives in sheltered accommodation with a lovely communal garden. But she was telling me that when she first moved in, how unkempt and untidy it was."

"Was?" I queried.

Monica laughed. "You don't know Aunt Joan! When she discovered that it was no-one's particular responsibility to care for it, she started doing what was needed herself — clearing litter, weeding, whatever she could manage. Even I became involved, putting in some bedding plants and very soon, every resident became involved, doing what they could."

I am reminded that Nobel Peace Prize winner Kofi Annan was right when he observed: "If we are to go on living together on this earth, we must all be responsible for it."

And if we did, what a beautiful place it would be!

May

HAVE you ever found a feather,
Found a feather on your way?
It means an angel's near you,
Watching o'er you, so they say.
Yet though that thought's uplifting,
And believe it if you will,
I'm sure the truth is better,
Just as real, and greater still.
For no-one needs a feather,
Needs a feather just to show
That angels hover near us,
Always watching as we go.
So if you find a feather,
Though your spirits it may cheer,
Just remember loving angels
Are always – always – near.

                Margaret Ingall

THE most effective stroke in any tennis match is the "ace." It takes nerve and accuracy to place the ball just inside the line so the opponent doesn't have much opportunity to hit it back.

Shots like that prompted one tennis fan to voice an opinion that surely also applies to life outside the tennis courts. "You know," he said, "the one who serves properly rarely loses!"

Friday — **May 3**

DOUG'S not so sprightly now, but it doesn't stop him nurturing his vegetables and flowers to give away to anybody he thinks could benefit from them.

As Augustine of Hippo said: "Since you cannot do good to all, you are to pay special attention to those who, by the accidents of time, or place, or circumstances, are brought into closer connection with you."

It's an attitude to cultivate even if we don't have Doug's green fingers.

Saturday — **May 4**

HERE are a few encouraging words to recall when you are trying to accomplish something which is difficult to achieve: "Believe you can and you're halfway there."

Theodore Roosevelt

And remember, Rome wasn't built in a day!

Sunday — **May 5**

TONY, a professional speaker who appears regularly at a variety of functions, admits to being slightly nervous before giving a talk. To dispel this feeling, he always tells his audience an amusing story at the beginning and then, when everyone has had a good laugh, they relax — and so does he. By doing this, they establish a light-hearted entente of shared fun from which the rest of the talk can comfortably proceed.

Medical experts tell us that laughter relieves tension and stress, helps the immune system and relaxes muscles, among a host of other health-boosting properties. Today is World Laughter Day and the Rev Oliver Wilson wrote these apt words: "Laughter is God's hand on a troubled world."

"Blessed are ye that weep now: for ye shall laugh."

(Luke 6:21)

Capital Vista

Monday — *May 6*

ROBERT is a fan of American author Dan Zadra. One of his favourite quotes is: "Always know in your heart that you are far bigger than anything that can happen to you."

Robert held on to those words when he was injured in an accident and, later, had to give up work but he was determined to recover and find new employment. Against great odds, he even learned to walk and talk again.

Although he has to use a walking stick and speaks rather haltingly, he has found work close to home where he oversees a programme that employs disabled people. Robert manages their schedules and allocates duties such as sweeping up leaves and removing litter.

Robert loves his new job and knows he is uniquely equipped to understand and support the people he works with. As he often says: "If God calls you to it, He'll lead you through it."

Tuesday — *May 7*

"WHEN I was very young," Andrew told me. "It seems that my biggest ambition was to catch a rainbow in a bucket. I was most upset when I never managed to do so!"

Poor Andrew! Like many of us, he was so busy trying to achieve the impossible that he failed to be consoled by all the other wonderful things that are far more easily achieved. This reminds me of Nathaniel Hawthorne's comment in the 19th century:

"Happiness is like a butterfly which, when pursued, is always beyond our grasp, but which, if you will sit down quietly, may alight upon you."

May age and wisdom allow us all to appreciate both butterflies and rainbows!

Wednesday — **May 8**

THERE'S an old expression used by gardeners that tells us: "Cultivate Honesty for its seeds."

The plant called honesty is unique in that its "seed-heads" are flat, oval and translucent, like wonderful see-through leaves. They are sought after by flower arrangers who use them to add an interesting touch to their displays.

Of course, we should cultivate honesty in our personal lives as well. And the seeds of that particular trait, the interesting things it causes to flower in others — well, they are no less wonderful.

Thursday — **May 9**

WE should never throw up our hands in despair at the very time when just a little more effort, a little more patience, would bring success within our reach. As Abraham Lincoln once said:

"I am a slow walker but I never walk backwards."

Friday — **May 10**

A NEWSPAPER at the time called it "the ultimate impossibility!" Back in the 1930s, Johnny Longden was a jockey and one day in the middle of a race, his foot slipped from a stirrup.

He lurched to one side and was in real danger of falling off. The jockey beside him pushed him back up – but pushed too hard. Longden almost fell off the other side of his horse. Another jockey caught him and pushed him upright again. Amazingly, Longden won the race!

So, what is the ultimate impossibility? Well, with enough helping hands . . . nothing!

Saturday — *May 11*

COMPTON Mackenzie's dreams of becoming a successful author seemed doomed to failure. A collection of poems he had worked on for years had attracted little interest, and a play had proved a disappointment, too.

To consider his future, he went to stay in a quiet corner of the Cornish coast. One night he went for a walk on the cliffs, his mood one of despair. As he stared into the darkness, his eye was caught by a tiny glow-worm shining in the grass at his feet.

He took it as an omen, hurried back to his room and began to write the first of the many novels that made his name. The tiny glow-worm had given him the hope and determination he needed.

Sunday — *May 12*

A MOTHER wanted her son to remember something at school. He kept repeating, half-heartedly, that he would try. "Don't try — remember!" she insisted.

Displeased at being held to account the boy tried a compromise. "All right, then. I'll try *and* I'll remember!"

In other words he would do what his mother wanted but he still wished it to sound like he was calling the shots.

We have all kinds of ways of asserting our independence in life: our worship might be the intermittent kind, our truth might be just a little flexible at times, but just like that youngster with his mother, someone wiser has already told us the right thing to do. We just need to get over our stubbornness, remember we are loved — and do it!

"Walk in all the ways that the Lord your God has commanded you, so that you may live and prosper and prolong your days in the land you will possess."

(Deuteronomy 5:33)

Summer Reflections

Monday — **May 13**

*S*HARED joy is a double joy;
Shared sorrow is half a sorrow.

Swedish Proverb

Tuesday — **May 14**

*I*T'S the kind of a day
for mowing the lawn,
Or catching a glimpse
of the sunlight at dawn,
For sitting beside a
fast-flowing stream,
And watching the salmon
that fleetingly gleam.

It's the kind of a day
to listen to birds,
With the lowing of cattle
in cud-chewing herds,
Or the bleating of lambs
newly born that beguile,
By the edge of the field
and an old rustic stile.

It's the kind of a day
that instantly pleases,
As willow trees sway
in the sweet zephyr breezes,
So many treasures
that all interplay,
When you wake up
to this kind of a day.

Brian H. Gent

Wednesday — **May 15**

HAVE you noticed the posters reminding us that it is Christian Aid Week? The sight of them prompted me to find out more about the origins of this event, and it didn't take long to discover that it all began in the aftermath of the Second World War.

The plight of so many European refugees touched the hearts and minds of British and Irish church leaders who, under the name of Christian Reconstruction in Europe, set out to alleviate the suffering. A few years later they decided to widen their area of assistance, to change their name, and initiate the first Christian Aid Week.

Today, more than 60 years on, the organisation is still going from strength to strength.

Thursday — **May 16**

THE famous writer Johann Wolfgang von Goethe, who was born in Frankfurt-on-Main in 1749, wrote: "He is happiest be he king or peasant, who finds peace in his home."

A good thought for today – or any day.

Friday — **May 17**

IN these days of digital photography George still prefers to develop his films the old-fashioned way – in a dark room he made in his garden shed.

It was there that he passed on his favourite photography tip. It wasn't anything about cameras or exposures or lenses, it was these thought-provoking words:

"A photographer knows the best photos are developed in darkness. So, if you look around and your life seems dark, you can be sure God is using it to develop a beautiful picture for you."

Saturday — **May 18**

*O*UR way is not a grassy path
   With sunbeams all around,
But rather like a mountain track
Where boulders can be found.

The path of life is often steep
And clouds obscure the view,
But keep on climbing, mile by mile,
Towards a sky of blue.

The path goes onward, forward, up
To where your hopes can soar,
And one day, from the mountain top
You'll see the sun once more!

                    Iris Hesselden

Sunday — **May 19**

IN 1820 when Fanny Crosby — later van Alstyne — was only six weeks old, she became blind. In later life, her poetry became well known and she also wrote hymns set to tunes sent to her by various music publishers.

Fanny interpreted her blindness as a channel God used to make her life's work possible. By choice, she lived in a rented room in the slums of New York, and was a familiar figure on the streets of Manhattan and Brooklyn, helping others. When publishers sent her gifts and money, she gave them away.

Fanny's hymns became well loved. Composer Phoebe Knapp played a tune to Fanny one day which she had composed.

Asking what the notes said, Fanny's reply was, "Blessed assurance!" The words duly followed for this favourite hymn, one of several thousand in total.

THE FRIENDSHIP BOOK

Monday — **May 20**

THE dog-eared hardback book had been printed in 1944. It had seen several owners in its long life and inside was a stamp saying it conformed to the "Book Production War Economy Standard", so it had been printed during wartime austerity when paper was rationed.

This book still remained inspirational to me. The good heart of the author shone through, no matter how economical the body of the book. What a pleasant surprise!

And it's an even more wonderful surprise when we find the same in people.

Tuesday — **May 21**

I'VE been reading about a Tornado that has been sweeping through the UK. No, not the kind of violent wind that wreaks havoc and destruction, but a far more welcome kind.

The Tornado I'm talking about is a brand-new steam locomotive, the first to be built since steam became obsolete. Built by whom, you may be wondering? By a group of dedicated enthusiasts who refused to believe anyone who told them it couldn't be done.

I hope that, like me, you enjoy hearing such inspiring stories. Whatever your dream, may it also run full steam to success.

Wednesday — **May 22**

THE Canadian physicist Sir William Osler once voiced this opinion: "Nothing will sustain you more potently than the power to recognise in your humdrum routine (as perhaps it may seem) the true poetry of life."

So, the next time your daily routine starts to seem a bit humdrum, look for the poem within. You may be pleasantly surprised.

Thursday – *May 23*

THE 14th-century Persian poet Hafiz addressed his students saying: "The subject tonight is love."

Perfectly acceptable, his students probably thought.

"And for tomorrow night as well," he added.

Some may have sighed, others may have been content. The happy ones would have been most in tune with their tutor who added: "As a matter of fact, I know of no better topic for us all to discuss until we die."

Love – it is that wonderful!

Friday – *May 24*

IF, like me, you're occasionally tempted to feel gloomy about the state of the world, one sure way of raising spirits is to think of the many wonderful people who make us feel good about humanity. They come from every century, every rung of the social ladder, and every part of the globe.

The one thing that unites them all is their belief that goodness will always triumph. As Martin Luther King Jr once said: "Even if I knew that tomorrow the world would go to pieces, I would still plant my apple tree."

And that's the sort of attitude that will always be fruitful.

Saturday – *May 25*

THE Celts didn't separate God from the everyday world. Instead they carried God with them into each part of their daily life.

To them, there was nothing that couldn't be made special by remembering God's presence – preparing food, feeding the hens, mending a fishing net. I like that, even though I often forget and leave God behind in church on a Sunday. I'll try my best to remember the Celts and do the same as them.

Sunday — *May 26*

WHEN husband Sam became ill Rosie found it difficult not to worry. Then one day she came across these words by Ralph Waldo Emerson:

"For each new morning with its light, Father, we thank Thee. For rest and shelter of the night, Father, we thank Thee."

She began to find a sense of peace and joy she'd never before experienced — Sam noticed and followed her example. They both later credited his recovery to the warm, gentle atmosphere of serenity that permeated their home.

"It is good to give thanks to the Lord and to sing praises to your name, O Most High, to declare your loving kindness in the morning and your faithfulness every night . . ."

(Psalms 92:1)

Monday — *May 27*

OUR friend Dorothy told the Lady of the House that when she was first introduced to computers, a young friend showed her a search facility that could supposedly answer all her questions.

I'm not sure how serious Dorothy was when she typed in these words: "How is my friend Agnes really doing after her operation?"

Her helper taught her a lot about the Internet, but I think Dorothy may have taught her something as well in turn; no search engine can ever compare with a friend's caring heart.

Tuesday — *May 28*

YOU know those people who always seem to be able to see the best in any situation, no matter how challenging? Well, even they could surely take lessons in optimism from the 17th-century Japanese poet Mizuta Masahide who wrote: "My barn having burned down, I now have a better view of the rising moon."

Now that's what I call really looking on the bright side!

Heavenly Heights

Wednesday — *May 29*

MUSK is one of the most expensive perfumes in the world, worth four times its weight in gold. The stag that produces it, according to ancient Sanskrit poetry, also finds the scent captivating.

One whiff of it in the air and the stag will spend days, wander many miles, and exhaust himself trying to find the scent's source. But of course, he is the source of the scent!

But before we laugh, let's make sure we're not doing the same thing, searching for happiness by looking for things outside ourselves when the secret of true happiness lies within.

Thursday — *May 30*

"IT was just a small thing," Sandra said, "but it really made my day." She was describing the moment when her young granddaughter, Hannah sitting with her in the garden had discovered a ladybird and watched entranced as it crawled along her finger.

"Such a tiny incident," Sandra recalled. "But seeing her face light up with wonder cheered me up for the rest of the day — and made me realise just how much our lives are enhanced by such little jewels of joy."

Let's make sure we don't miss any such jewels that come our way!

Friday — *May 31*

NORIO Ohga, who was credited with pioneering CD technology, had one requirement – a CD must be able to store all of Beethoven's 9th Symphony. Ohga wanted the world to be able to enjoy longer piece of recorded music uninterrupted for the first time.

Isn't it nice to know that even in the world of technology artistry still has far more influence than any of us might imagine?

June

FROM our old friend Mary's treasured collection of quotes about friendship she would like to share these favourite thoughts with you today:

"The secret of friendship is being a good listener."

"A true friend is someone you can trust with all your secrets."

"A true friend wants nothing more from you than the pleasure of your company."

"Friendship is a candle whose flame glows brighter when the hour is darker."

IN 1931 Archie moved to the Highlands for the good of his health. He was a doctor with ambitions as a writer, but when his first literary attempts failed he told a local farmer that he planned to give up.

"I've been working on this bog all my days," the farmer said, "and never made a pasture out of it yet. But I can't help but dig, for my father knew and I know that if you only dig for long enough a pasture can be made here."

A. J. Cronin — Archie — went on to sell millions of books, but don't you think that farmer's bog is a bit like daily life? A fertile pasture can be made if we don't give up, no matter how much we may feel discouraged at times.

"You need to persevere so that when you have done the will of God, you will receive what he has promised."

(Hebrews 10:36)

Monday — *June 3*

HOW do you change a life? With the gifts you have. Music teacher Peter probably didn't think the lessons he gave at a reform school would do much good. Most of the boys there had already been in trouble with the law and would, perhaps, get into even more. What difference could music lessons make?

Well, one of those boys was called Louis Armstrong. Peter certainly changed Satchmo's life!

How do you change a life? You take the gifts you have, you share them – and let God do the rest.

Tuesday — *June 4*

ARTHUR used to be employed on a big estate. It was his job to keep acres and acres of ornamental gardens in tip-top condition. These days, though, he has his allotment. It's well laid out as you might expect and productive, but ... I hesitated to ask ... wasn't it a bit of a come-down after all these years working on the estate?

Arthur considered my question for a moment, and then agreed that there might be something in it.

"Gardens come in all sizes," he said, "but ask those who work in them; no matter how long the plot is, or how wide, you'll find they generally reach all the way up to Heaven – and that's big enough for me!"

Wednesday — *June 5*

WHEN one door of happiness closes, another opens, but often we look so long at the closed door that we do not see the one that has been opened for us.

Helen Keller

Thursday — **June 6**

THE best remedy for those who are afraid, lonely or unhappy is to go outside, somewhere where they can be quiet, alone with the heavens, nature and God. Because only then does one feel that all is as it should be and that God wishes to see people happy, amidst the simple beauty of nature.

Anne Frank

Friday — **June 7**

IN the clear, whole light of morning,
While the world moves gently,
I go to the trees.
They are glad and strong;
Maple, birch, oak, pine,
Tall,
Oh, tall,
Tossing leafy crowns
At His feet.
Their praise whispers on the wind,
Building to a thousand silvered notes,
Then fading to a sigh of shivered adoration.
They reach for Him,
Tall,
Oh, tall,
To their Father,
Their Maker
And sing —
Hymns that mingle
High and pure
With my own.

Rachel Wallace-Oberle

Saturday — *June 8*

WHEN American science fiction writer Robert Heinlein was asked on a radio show what he believed, he decided to talk, not about religion, but about some less obvious beliefs. He affirmed his belief in his neighbours, in the goodness of strangers and then the honest craft of working men and women.

"Take a look around you," he said. "There were never enough bosses to check up on all that work. These things were built level and square by craftsmen who were honest in their bones."

As our friend Chris walked around the day after she read this, looking at office blocks and canals, railways and restaurants, houses and hospitals, she couldn't help but think of the thousands of unsupervised decisions that were made "square and right". And, like Mr Heinlein, she also gave thanks that most of the people we depend upon are "honest in their bones".

Sunday — *June 9*

COUNTLESS dramatisations and popular films have been made of his books — writer and university professor C.S. Lewis was a successful man by any standards. However, towards the end of his life he once asked: "If God had answered all the silly prayers I have prayed in my life, where would I be now?"

Most of us have prayed and at times have not received the answer we were hoping for. But remember, God is the author of our lives – and won't let our momentary desires deflect Him from writing our happy ever after.

"Praise be to God, who has not rejected my prayer or withheld his love from me!" (Psalm 66:20)

Monday — *June 10*

THE medieval Persian poet Saadi once gave voice to a lump of clay that had fallen into a garden. The garden had wilted with the passage of time but the clay still remembered how it had been.

"I am not the rose," the lump of clay said. "But I have lived near the rose."

The lump of clay felt it was somehow better for having lived near beauty. And because of that the rose lived on, even if only in memory.

Beauty lifts us all up and, no matter how fleetingly it is in our lives, we never have to let it go.

Tuesday — *June 11*

HERE are some wise words from the 16th-century English philosopher and statesman Francis Bacon, which seem just as relevant to us today:

"If a man be gracious and courteous to strangers, it shows he is a citizen of the world, and that his heart is no island cut off from other lands, but a continent that joins to them."

Wednesday — *June 12*

GEORGE Meredith enjoyed success as a writer in the Victorian era, but he also knew the meaning of hardship. His mother died when he was five and later, his wife left him for another man. So he experienced a life with equal shares of happiness and sadness, like many of us.

But he hinted at his conviction that all would work out well in the end. It's a thought we might borrow when life does not go as smoothly as we would like. He wrote these moving words:

"I feel sure that whatever happens to this battered old cage of mine, the little bird inside will be all right."

Thursday — *June 13*

"I WAS fed up with my job on the pier turnstile," Rob said. "Tourists often complained that their walk out to sea had been a waste of time, that there was nothing to see, and some of them even asked for their money back. Yet they were on holiday and supposed to be enjoying themselves.

"I found myself beginning to agree with them until one day something made me change my attitude and make my work much more worthwhile."

"What happened?" I asked.

"A party of smiling day-trippers returned from the end of the pier and glowingly thanked me for their experience. They felt invigorated by the sea breeze, the ozone, the sound of the waves, the call of the seagulls. And do you know something? They were all visually impaired."

May we learn to appreciate, too, those things that we would perhaps otherwise take for granted.

Friday — *June 14*

MY thought for today comes from the treasured and much-read diary which was kept by Great-Aunt Louisa, children's writer and artist.

"As this beautiful summer's day draws to a close, I think I will write in my diary these words by the Venerable Bede of Jarrow: *Life is a beautiful and strange winged creature that appears at a window, flies quickly through the banquet hall and is gone.*"

These thoughts from many centuries ago by the biographer of St Cuthbert remind us that we should make the most of every precious day.

Beside Great-Aunt Louisa's entry is a delicately drawn miniature watercolour of a winged fairy-like creature flying through a casement window.

Saturday — **June 15**

IT'S good to travel light through life,
Too much can weigh you down,
So cast away the tiresome things
That make you fret and frown.
Abandon grumps and silly gripes,
Forget the fears that blight,
If you just hold the things you love,
Your heart's forever light

Margaret Ingall

Sunday — **June 16**

CHARLOTTE Elliot was visiting friends in London and met the Swiss evangelist and hymn writer Cesar Malan. While seated at supper, he asked if Charlotte was a Christian. Taken aback, she replied that she would rather not talk about it.

However, it proved a turning point. Meeting Cesar Malan again she confessed that ever since he had spoken to her she had wanted to come to Christ, but she did not know how to find him.

"Come just as you are," he told her.

Pondering his words, Charlotte decided to write a song for those like herself, characterised by a tenderness of feeling and a simple deep devotion. She wrote "Just As I Am", which is still a favourite hymn today.

Monday — **June 17**

AMERICAN comedian Jonathan Winters once quipped: "I couldn't wait for success, so I went ahead without it." It's only human nature to want other people's encouragement, but if we're too timid and don't press on without it, we may turn back without ever achieving anything. So let's try to be like Jonathan Winters. After all, if we believe in ourselves, it's much more likely that everyone else will too.

Tuesday — **June 18**

"**D**O Not Disturb." When Ella and Brian arrived late and tired at their holiday hotel, they made sure that they hung that sign on their door before they went to bed. But they hadn't bargained for a mistaken telephone alarm call from the reception desk at 6 o'clock the following morning.

"We couldn't stay cross for long," Ella recalled with a smile. "For when we looked out the window we were rewarded by the most beautiful sunrise over the sea. If we had slept on undisturbed, we'd have missed it completely."

It's perhaps a timely reminder that however much we might prefer a quiet life, a little disturbance now and then can be quite beneficial!

Wednesday — **June 19**

*J*UNE and July come hand in hand,
The lovely ladies of the year,
Their perfume carried on the breeze,
Their beauty spreading far and near.
Adorned with roses, pinks and stocks,
They fill the gardens everywhere,
With scent of grass so newly mown
And sometimes, wood smoke on the air.

And though some days they bring a storm
With thunder and with heavy rain,
We, like the earth, can feel refreshed
Their loveliness will still remain.
The carnivals and garden fêtes,
So many things we shall recall,
In city or in country town
As this high summer touches all.

Iris Hesselden

Thursday — *June 20*

IF you happen to be in Kensington Gardens in London during the evening and you approach the statue of Peter Pan from the west, you might notice a wonderful transformation. Around Peter's feet dance little birds and animals, all made of bronze. The metal has weathered over the years until it looks almost black, but the heads of the little creatures often shine like gold.

That's because generations of children have reached out in affection and gently stroked those little heads, polishing them up to a golden shine.

Now, if love and tenderness can do that to metal …

Friday — *June 21*

IN the 1930s, George Nissen invented trampolines. He produced them, promoted them and later, trampolining became an Olympic sport.

The idea had come to him when watching trapeze artists in circuses. After they had finished dazzling the crowds with their exploits, they would often jump into the safety nets. Those with a little more flair might somersault or back-flip as they bounced. And that started young George thinking …

The safety nets were never supposed to be a part of the act, but the trapeze artists added a little extra. Why not try putting a little extra bounce into your life — you never know what might spring from it!

Saturday — *June 22*

NO love, no friendship, can cross the path of our destiny without leaving some mark on it forever.

Francois Mauriac

Sunday — *June 23*

THERE are some people in this world whose courage you simply can't help but admire. Take Bear Grylls, for example, who, having broken his back in three places as a young man in a disastrous parachute jump, was so determined to recover that not only did he return to parachute jumping, but also went on to further adventures such as leading a team across the North Atlantic and Arctic Ocean in a small boat.

He also became the youngest Briton to reach the summit of Mount Everest.

Yet even he is more than willing to admit he relies on help. "It takes a proud man to say he needs nothing," he once said, "and for me my Christian faith has always been my backbone."

There is one book he is never without, his New Testament: "an old friend which I have taken on every major expedition I have ever done." And his favourite verse? Well, unsurprising perhaps, that comes from Matthew 28:20: "I am with you even unto the end of the world."

Words that can bring comfort to us all, wherever our journeys may take us.

Monday — *June 24*

THE Lady of the House has a friend who has always had a busy job and a rather hectic life at home, too, but Jane always has a smile for everyone she meets. We found this greeting on a birthday card for her which we thought was especially appropriate:

"If life is a rollercoaster, you might as well sit at the front and enjoy the ride."

She certainly does that and yet she still finds time to share her sense of fun and optimism with all those around her. Something for us all to think about when the pace of living is hectic.

Woodland Wonder

Tuesday — *June 25*

WHEN Brenda opened her front door to our old friend Mary, she was brandishing a tin of polish. "I don't like dusting very much," she explained. "But at least it doesn't take long — unlike sorting out all the old family photos, which is something I'm doing for my grandchildren. Even though it's more fun, I'm not sure I'll ever be finished!"

Her words reminded me of a quote by Bruce Barton, who once said: "All life is immortality; all work eternally significant. Every worthwhile man who ever has lived has made plans bigger than his own lifetime."

Whether your particular job for today is small or part of an ongoing big project, I hope you can derive a special sense of enjoyment from it.

Wednesday — *June 26*

THE Foundation for International Development Assistance is a small Canadian organisation that works with the poor in rural Haiti. Through agriculture cooperatives, staff teach farmers how to produce and store healthy crops, as well as focusing on literacy skills, conflict resolution and sound business practices.

The success of FIDA's work is due to strong relationships — the farmers trust and work closely with staff, who actually live with them for short periods of time in remote mountainous regions.

Every piece of FIDA's correspondence carries this ethos of the cooperatives: *If we work hand in hand, we can go far. We must trust each other because we need each other to go on.*

These are powerful words to live by. In this world, which seems to grow smaller each day, we are all neighbours responsible for the wellbeing of one another.

Thursday — **June 27**

EIGHT-YEAR-OLD Avril loves to go hop-skipping down the road outside her home. But one winter's afternoon a violent thunderstorm seemed to come out of nowhere, and her mother, realising her daughter had disappeared from view, jumped into the family car and drove slowly down the road in search of her.

The storm had by then reached new heights, with thunderclaps and flashes of lightning, when she suddenly caught sight of her daughter stopping every so often, turning her face to the heavens, and giving a beaming smile.

"Avril, whatever are you doing?" asked her mother as she quickly approached her.

"Oh, don't worry, Mummy," Avril replied. "God wants me to give Him my biggest smile – look, that's His new flash camera and He's taking my photograph every two minutes!"

Friday — **June 28**

PHILOSOPHY from a puddle — whatever am I talking about today? Well, it was shallow and wide enough to cover the path Dave and Linda were walking along. Like many others before them, judging by the muddy footprints and bicycle tyre tracks, Linda decided to walk carefully along the sodden grass verge.

But Dave just walked on regardless, smiling at Linda slipping and sliding around.

"You can hesitate and skirt around it," he said. "You might get safely through, but you might get muddy, you might slip and you might fall. But if you have a stout pair of shoes and tackle it head on, you'll get safely to the other side and your shoes might even be cleaner than they were before."

You know, it occurs to me that if you swap faith for those stout shoes, you have a sound philosophy for life.

Saturday — *June 29*

IF a man does not make new acquaintances as he advances through life, he will soon find himself alone. A man should keep his friendships in constant repair.

Samuel Johnson

Sunday — *June 30*

THANK you, Lord, for simple pleasures;
Forests lush, and meadows green.
Thank you for the wealth of harvest;
Summer's blush and dawning's steam.
Thank you for the precious sunlight,
And the sweet escape of rain.
Thank you for each new day dawning.
Hope afresh and life again.
Thank you for the snow in Winter,
When the plants can rest awhile.
For the beauty in each flower,
Where we surely see your smile.
Thank you for your words of comfort;
For the joy in your embrace.
Thank you for your understanding;
Patience and amazing grace.
Thank you for your hand of friendship
When our heart is sad and low.
Thank you for the quiet moments
Where your living waters flow.
Thank you Lord, for all your blessings.
For your son, who conquered sin.
For your love, total and binding.
For your light that shines within us.

Mo Crawshaw

**Clearly
Cloudless**

July

FLOWERS, and all things green and growing, give a great deal of pleasure to so many of us. The American poet Celia Thaxter celebrated the tranquil peace of a garden at the dawn of a new day in these words:

"When in those fresh mornings I go into my garden before anyone is awake, I go for the time being into perfect happiness. In this hour, divinely fresh and still, the fair face of every flower salutes me with a silent joy that fills me with infinite content; each gives its color, its grace, its perfume and enriches me with the consummation of its beauty."

TOO much hustle, too much bustle
Frantic speeding everywhere,
Too much hurry, too much worry
Never getting anywhere.

Through our lives we go on rushing
Really we should take a pause –
Always anxious, always fussing
Never trying to seek the cause.

Why then do we live our life span
Frittering our time away?
Why not stop and then take stock
Of what we do with each new day?
                    Kathleen Gillum

Wednesday — **July 3**

VISITING Mark's home one afternoon, the Lady of the House and I remarked on the several walls of bookshelves fully stacked from floor to ceiling with volumes of all sizes.

"Well, I admit I haven't read them all," he said, "but I hope to one day, and there are many old friends here I'd like to read again and again. Do you know, I'm comforted by their very presence — I expect great things from them when I finally turn their pages."

He appreciated that his collection of books was there, readily available if needed, old and trusted, reliable, a source of wonder and pleasure. "Just like loyal, reassuring, old friends," he added.

Hollywood actress Shirley MacLaine's words about long friendships echo this feeling: "We are there for each other, even if we are not always seen."

Thursday — **July 4**

"LIVE your beliefs and you can turn the world around. So said Henry Thoreau.

Well, they are wonderful words, you may be thinking, but can this really be done? Certainly our friend Louise would have had some reservations a few years ago. As a busy mother, her free time was extremely limited, but she did what she could and filled a shoebox for a Romanian orphan.

The following year she filled several, and persuaded friends and neighbours to do likewise. The year after that she was helping to organise their collection and, now that her children are older, they all pay regular visits to that distant orphanage, renewing friendships, and making life a little better for many children.

So, do you still doubt that we can turn the world around? I don't — not if we all push together!

Friday — *July 5*

SALLY'S physiotherapist likes to inspire her patients by decorating her office with quotes and sayings and to keep things interesting, she regularly adds to them. One afternoon, Sally caught sight of this newly posted gem and nodded in agreement:

"There is nothing so bad that it couldn't be worse, but there is nothing so good that it couldn't be better."

Wise words for us all to keep in mind, don't you think?

Saturday — *July 6*

IN one of the old King Arthur legends we hear of the brave knights Percival and Gawain. They have been on a long quest through the forest, and Gawain's page has kept his armour spotless, polished shiny bright.

But Percival doesn't have a page and his armour has rusted to the point where it could never again be like Gawain's. Yet as the setting sun shone "full upon the knights twain, the one did seem all shining with light, and the other all to glow with ruddy fire."

We may not all be perfect as the world defines perfection but all it takes is the right light to show the beauty in everyone.

Sunday — *July 7*

ST BASIL had more to do with gardening than just sharing his name with a herb! He was one of the early organisers of communal monastic living, teaching young friars how to make their community self-sufficient, often through growing their own produce.

One of his gardening tips, given around 1700 years ago, is still valid today. "He who sows courtesy reaps friendship," St Basil said. "And he who plants kindness gathers love."

"They sowed fields and planted vineyards that yielded a fruitful harvest." (Psalm 107:37)

Monday — **July 8**

ISABELLE has a reputation for being unflappable. The Lady of the House has known her for many years and doesn't recall her ever losing her calm demeanour for more than a few seconds.

When Isabelle was asked about her secret for staying so calm, she smiled and said: "When in doubt, sit it out."

Wise words to take into many a situation, every day!

Tuesday — **July 9**

SONG OF THE WIND

I HEAR the wind whispering,
Then growing strong
And he touches my heart
With the sound of his song.
He sings of the moors
And the heather in bloom,
The mosses and bracken,
The bright, golden broom.
He tells of wild places,
The curlew in flight,
The silence of evening,
The bright stars alight.
He sings of the moonlight
And frost on the air,
The crags silhouetted,
Rocks rugged and bare,
The wind brings me memories,
Filling the day,
And I follow that moorland path,
So far away.

Iris Hesselden

Wednesday — **July 10**

MANY years ago the entertainer Danny Thomas was having financial difficulties. He hadn't worked in weeks and his wife was in hospital having their first child. He needed money to cover medical costs and had scarcely anything.

Danny went to church and begged for help, promising God he would establish something to honour Him. When Danny went home, the phone rang and he was offered a job and was even given money in advance. That is why Danny decided to establish the St Jude Hospital for Children in 1962.

Henry Ward Beecher had this interesting perspective on prayer: "I pray on the principle that wine knocks the cork out of a bottle. There is an inward fermentation and there must be a vent."

Danny Thomas would surely have agreed.

Thursday — **July 11**

WITH a job that takes Don all over the country, we were sad rather than surprised to hear that Sandra and her husband would soon be moving house again.

"What are your best tips on packing?" the Lady of the House asked.

"Never pack the kettle and cups too deeply!" answered Sandra at once. "And secondly, do make sure that photos of friends and family are always kept handy. If you're feeling a bit lost and lonely in a new environment, it's good to be surrounded by pictures of all the people who are fond of you, and wishing you well. In fact, it often helps to give me the confidence to go out and make new friends."

We'll miss Don and Sandra, but haven't any doubt that they will soon be as valued in their new community as they have been in ours.

Friday — *July 12*

THE Lady of the House was given a small calendar which also served as a bookmark. The quotations were all about the qualities of friendship and one in particular by Donna Roberts had great appeal:

"A friend knows the song in my heart and sings it to me when my memory fails."

How fortunate we are if we have such a friend. We should always cherish friendship and try to be a good friend to others in return.

Saturday — *July 13*

NINETEENTH-century poet, Sarah Williams, lived in the shadow of ill-health for most of her brief life, but she left us a legacy of memorable writing. One of my favourites is "The Old Astronomer To His Pupil", and I would love to share with you this small excerpt:

Though my soul may set in darkness,
It will rise in perfect light.
I have loved the stars too fondly
To be fearful of the night.

Heartfelt words from a brave and inspirational writer.

Sunday — *July 14*

IN a world that often tries to make each day of the week the same as every other day, we have a choice. We can go that way, or we can follow the example of 17th-century essayist Joseph Addison and aim to make Sunday different: "Sunday clears away the rust of the whole week."

"For in six days the Lord made the heavens and the earth, the sea, and all that is in them, but he rested on the seventh day. Therefore the Lord blessed the Sabbath day and made it holy." (Exodus 20:11)

Monday — *July 15*

AMERICAN astronaut Neil Armstrong was Commander of Apollo 11 and the first man to walk on the moon in July, 1969. He said: "Accomplishing a goal is not as important as the person you become accomplishing it."

Our young friend Henry often thinks of these profound words as he trains for long-distance running. Despite weather conditions or how he feels, he laces up his running shoes and heads outside, determined to log his required miles for the week.

There are times when he feels tired and dispirited, he says, or the weather turns against him and he feels like giving up. But that's when a spark of resilience flares and he determinedly focuses on his goal. And all the while he keeps Armstrong's inspiring words firmly in mind.

Is there something you long to achieve? Don't hesitate! You may well exceed your expectations and be surprised at who you become along the way.

Tuesday — *July 16*

SAVOUR the moments of joy that appear,
For all too soon, they'll disperse, disappear,
But if you enfold them with care in your heart,
The memory will stay and will then be a part
Of contentment and promise of joys yet to be,
And in holding them close, you'll find tranquillity.
Chrissy Greenslade

Wednesday — *July 17*

THE greatest good you can do for another is not just share your riches, but to reveal to him, his own.
Benjamin Disraeli

Thursday — *July 18*

"THE time to try is the trying time." What does that mean? Well, anyone can be an optimist when things are going well. But when life is hard, when the days are short and the weather bleak – that's a time of opportunity for the genuine optimist, or the man or woman who aspires to be the real deal.

That's when you get to rise above the easy option of complaining and search for the good that is always there, no matter how well hidden. In finding it you can often bring out the best in people who didn't know they had it in them.

The time to try is the trying time.

Friday — *July 19*

YOU'LL find her in the meadow
Or down a country lane,
And there's no doubt about it
Her charms will never wane.

Sometimes in parks and gardens
You'll see her upturned face,
And if it takes her fancy,
Your prized lawn she will grace.
One thing is for certain,
She displays tenacity.

The lesson there for everyone
Is very plain to see.
So surely she's the jewel
In nature's summer crown,
For everything seems brighter
When Miss Daisy comes to town!
              Brian H. Gent

*Saturday — **July 20***

TREAT your friends as you do your pictures and place them in their best light.

Jennie Jerome Churchill

*Sunday — **July 21***

ARE you feeling a little downhearted about your present situation, or uncertain about how things will work out for you? Even if there can be no instant solution, I'd like to remind you of these words to be found in Joshua 1:9:

"Be strong and courageous. Do not be terrified, do not be discouraged, for the Lord your God will be with you wherever you go."

A thought which will surely bring comfort.

*Monday — **July 22***

APPARENTLY a hotel in Singapore once offered an all-you-can-eat breakfast buffet and if you finished your meal in under 30 minutes you paid half price.

Our well-travelled friend Chris said: "I made a saving that day, but I lost my decorum feeling under pressure to eat so much and so quickly. I lost my dignity, my civility and — would you believe it — my appetite for the rest of the day because I had such bad heartburn!"

A bargain may seem tempting but watch out for the hidden costs!

Let's take time out of our busy schedules to consider and appreciate the important things in life — thinking of others, getting to know people, how we are going to live each day to the full and don't forget that a leisurely breakfast makes a good start to the day ahead.

Tuesday — *July 23*

A PATH that has no obstacles
Seems tempting in extreme,
We stroll along, we take our time,
We dawdle and we dream.
But sadly, there's one little snag
Which always will befall:
A path that holds no challenges
Leads nowhere much at all.

Margaret Ingall

Wednesday — *July 24*

EVERYONE loves a friend on whom they know they can rely, but it would be a shame if that meant we take them for granted. That's why I like this quote:

"Do not keep the alabaster boxes of your love and tenderness sealed up until your friends are dead. Fill their lives with sweetness. Speak approving, cheering words while their ears can hear them and while their hearts can be thrilled by them." Henry Ward Beecher

Thursday — *July 25*

KIND hearts are the gardens,
Kind thoughts are the roots,
Kind words are the flowers,
Kind deeds are the fruits,
Take care of your garden,
And keep out the weeds,
Fill it with sunshine,
Kind words and deeds.

I wonder if you have come across this verse written by the 19th-century poet Henry Wadsworth Longfellow? We should never hesitate to be kind – there is never too much kindness in the world.

Friday — **July 26**

MOST people would like to give more to the worthy charities we hear about. Or maybe there's work to be done in the local community. Or perhaps it's one person we know of who needs a helping hand.

Sometimes we can help in practical ways, sometimes we aren't in that position. The dilemma and the answer are summed up in this proverb which advises: "If you have much, give of your wealth; if you have little, give of your heart."

Saturday — **July 27**

"YOU must be feeling so pleased with yourself!" I congratulated Colin, who had just passed his driving test at the first attempt.

"Well, not just with myself," he answered. "After all, if it hadn't been for the patience of my instructor, my parents who allowed me to practise in their car, and my friends who kept testing me on the Highway Code . . ." He grinned. "Well, you can see I didn't do it all on my own."

His realisation made me think of these words from George Bernard Shaw: "We are all dependent upon one another, every soul of us on Earth."

Sunday — **July 28**

HARRY doesn't believe we need to kneel down to pray. "God doesn't need to see me humbled," he said.

So, how did he pray? "Oh, on my knees," he replied.

Seeing me at a loss Harry explained: "There are parts of me that are less than perfect, believe it or not; parts that are vain, independent, doubting. When I kneel they have to as well. And it does me good to see them humbled."

"Come, let us bow down in worship, let us kneel before the Lord our Maker." (Psalm 95:6)

Monday — *July 29*

LIFE follows an ever-changing pattern and many of us do not find it easy to adapt to change. The 19th-century writer and poet John Henry Newman had this to say:

"In a higher world it is otherwise; but here below to live is to change, and to be perfect is to have changed often."

Perhaps those of us who find change especially difficult should remember that the way things work out may not be to our liking at first but can be for the better in the long run.

Tuesday — *July 30*

HE was known in the 1980s as B.A. Baracus, one of the stars of the hit series, "The A-Team." The initials B.A. stood for "Bad Attitude", but in real life Mr T has a much better attitude. He went on to do another television show where he helped inspire people in difficult situations.

When asked what he'd learned through doing the show, he replied: "People just need a little push sometimes – sometimes it's just a pat on the back. That's what I try to bring. I bring the love."

It doesn't require celebrity, it doesn't need money and each of us, regardless of our situation, can do it. As B.A. might have said: "I pity the fool who can't say, 'I bring the love!' "

Wednesday — *July 31*

JOHN Dewey (1859–1952) was an American philosopher, psychologist and educational reformer and this is one of his many memorable observations: "To be fully alive, the future is not ominous but a promise; it surrounds the present like a halo."

I like these words with their cheerful, positive outlook on life and hope that you will find them inspiring, too. They are words for all seasons, well worth noting.

August

THERE'S beauty in the evening sky
A wash of blazing light
The colours intermingling
Before dissolving into night.
Lovely shades of tangerine
And cranberry and lemon
Apricot and cherry red
All the fruits of heaven.
A beacon at the end of day
For all the world to see
A winding down, a special time
Bringing peace and tranquillity.
                    Dorothy McGregor

THE Lady of the House put down her book with a smile. "Listen to this, Francis," she said. "It's a quote from our old friend Anon, describing a force that 'sees the invisible, feels the intangible, and achieves the impossible'. Can you guess what he's talking about?"

Could it have been Superman or a hero from a comic book? Before I could mull over any other possibilities, the Lady of the House interrupted, saying, "It's actually something quite straightforward. Anon was talking about hope."

Ah well, no-one can get it right all the time. And happily for us, hope is far more common and even more powerful than any comic book hero!

Saturday — *August 3*

JOE had been a hard worker all his life, so when poor health forced him into early retirement, he found it difficult to take it easy.

"It wasn't that I couldn't think of anything interesting to do," he said, smiling. "But whatever I did, I always felt rather guilty that it wasn't more useful. Then I read some words which made me realise it was all just a matter of changing priorities."

"And those words were . . ?" I prompted.

Joe smiled. "It was a quote from Walter Rauschenbusch. He said: 'The real joy in life is in its play. Play is anything we do for the joy and love of doing it, apart from any profit, compulsion, or sense of duty. It is the real joy of living.'"

And if discovering the joy of living isn't invaluable, then I don't know what is!

Sunday — *August 4*

WHEN President Jimmy Carter appointed Sidney Rand as Ambassador to Norway, he knew he was promoting someone who really cared for people.

A tutor at St Olaf's College recalled Dr Rand's first day there. "I noticed that whenever someone stood to ask a question, Sidney would call on them by name. Then I had a question and I stood up, and he called on me by name — and we had never even met!"

Sidney Rand's example stayed with that tutor for decades afterwards. But how impressive would it have been if he had known the names of not only the entire faculty, but all the students, and all the inhabitants of the nearby town . . . and all of the birds, animals, insects, every blade of grass . . .

"Are not five sparrows sold for two pennies? Yet not one of them is forgotten by God. Indeed, the very hairs of your head are numbered." (Luke 12: 6-7)

Monday — *August 5*

ISAAC Walton, a 17th-century writer and philosopher, was once out walking with a friend when a heavy shower descended. He invited the friend to shelter under a high honeysuckle hedge.

"There we'll sit and sing," he said, "while this shower falls so gently upon the teeming earth, and gives yet a sweeter smell to the lovely flowers that adorn these verdant meadows."

Now, most of us caught out in inclement weather these days won't be smelling flowers and honeysuckle on verdant meadows, but won't we think a little more kindly of the rain knowing it still helps flowers and plants to thrive?

Tuesday — *August 6*

IT is not how much you do, but how much love you put into the doing that matters.   Mother Teresa

Wednesday — *August 7*

YOU know those little white stones that often dot black tarmac pavements? I'm sure you've often seen them but probably never given them much thought, although they perform a vital function.

Black tarmac heats up with the sun, then cools down at night. Eventually, the expansion and contraction causes cracking and without the stones there, the cracks might keep going. They might lengthen, widen, dirt would get in, weeds would grow and the weeds would lift the tarmac. But if the crack hits one of those little white stones — it stops!

Isn't it amazing how, in so many ways, a little light in the darkness stops everything from falling apart?

Thursday — *August 8*

OUR friend Betty was recalling her days in the Brownies and mentioned a song they used to sing to the tune of Auld Lang Syne. Why not sing along with these cheerful lines now?

A smile is such a funny thing,
It wrinkles up your face;
And when it's gone it's hard to find
Its secret hiding place.
But far more wonderful it is
To see what smiles can do.
I smile at you, you smile at me,
And so one smile makes two!

Friday — *August 9*

DURING this sunny season most of us enjoy gardening and being outdoors in the fresh air. Recently, the Lady of the House came across these quotes in a desk diary which reflect the pleasures of summer to be found close to home:

A garden is a friend you can visit any time.

Gardening is a way of showing that you believe in tomorrow.

Saturday — *August 10*

THERE can be few civilised Englishwomen whose name is so associated with murder as Agatha Christie. Happily, as we all know, her expertise in that deadly occupation was purely within the realms of fiction and, despite her love of creating lethal puzzles, she never underplayed the preciousness of life.

She was recorded as saying: "I like living. I have sometimes been wildly, despairingly, acutely miserable, racked with sorrow, but through it all I still know quite certainly that just to be alive is a grand thing."

Beyond These Shores

Sunday — *August 11*

A MAN who used to have a troubled life told me the best advice he ever had came from our old friend Mary. She told him to buy a pair of slippers!

"Pick comfortable ones," she had advised, "so you will wear them around the house a lot. Then, when it comes to bedtime, put them as far under your bed as you can."

Apparently Mary had smiled at his puzzled expression. Then she added these words: "And while you are down on your knees anyway …"

Buying those slippers, he tells me, has made all the difference!

"One day Jesus told his disciples a story to show that they should always pray and never give up." (Luke 18:1)

Monday — *August 12*

O NE sunny morning the Lady of the House found a ladybird – "the beetle of Our Lady" – on the hall carpet. Folklore tells of these beautiful creatures with their distinctive seven black spots as the Virgin Mary's messengers, the seven spots corresponding to her Seven Joys and Sorrows, and she was also often depicted wearing a red cloak in early paintings.

In the Hebrides of Scotland the ladybird's spots are often interpreted as symbols of the wounds of Christ. In general, they are also believed to be harbingers of good fortune and weather and are certainly good friends of keen gardeners. In many countries, including Turkey and Italy, seeing a ladybird is a time to make a wish or is a sign that a wish already made will soon be granted.

Summer with its balmy rose-scented days is here, a time when we will catch many glimpses of ladybirds when we are outdoors enjoying the seasonal beauty of nature.

Tuesday — **August 13**

OF all the changes over the past few years, perhaps the most encouraging is the increasing importance we are beginning to place upon the environment, although the idea that we should look after our world is certainly not a new one.

Chief Seattle, a Native American leader of the Suquamish and Duwamish tribes, was born around 1780, but even then knew the value of putting our own role into the right perspective. This is what he said:

"Humankind has not woven the web of life. We are but one thread within it. Whatever we do to the web, we do to ourselves. All things are bound together. All things connected."

Words to inspire every one of us.

Wednesday — **August 14**

LIFE has its moments of pure joy – cherish them and keep them close to your heart. They will sparkle like diamonds in your tapestry of memories and brighten less sunny times for, as the 18th century poet William Blake so rightly said: "Joy and woe are woven fine."

Thursday — **August 15**

CONAN O'Brien is one of the most successful presenters on television in the United States. His was a career he could never have foreseen and the experience has helped him to develop an interesting take on life.

"Nobody in life gets exactly what they thought they were going to get," he has commented. "But if you work really hard and you're kind amazing things will happen!"

Now, we may wonder which of these attributes are more important. Just to be safe, perhaps we could combine the two, because if you work hard at being kind, amazing things really will happen!

Friday — *August 16*

OUR friend Hannah is one of the kindest people we know, for when friends and neighbours are feeling poorly she is always among the first to send them a card, take them a bunch of flowers from her garden or run errands for them.

But Hannah herself doesn't realise the contribution she is making to the lives of others. She, like most of us, probably thinks that our lives revolve around great moments but great moments often catch us unawares, tenderly wrapped in what others may consider small ones.

When you show kindness to others, they may not remember exactly what you did or said but they will certainly remember how you made them feel.

Saturday — *August 17*

THE Lady of the House found this amusing quote when leafing through a magazine one day:

To keep love brimming in the loving cup, when you're wrong admit it and when you're right shut up.

How true!

Sunday — *August 18*

FOR most of us the name Ebenezer will conjure up images of the Dickens character Ebenezer Scrooge who was notoriously ungrateful for anything. But an Ebenezer was a monument raised in thanks by the biblical prophet Samuel and the name meant, "Thus far the Lord has helped us."

Let's not join Scrooge in saying, "Bah, humbug," to life and its blessings. Instead let's follow Samuel's example and take every opportunity we can to stop, look around and say thank you for the helping hands that got us here.

"Then Samuel took a stone and set it up between Mizpah and Shen. He named it Ebenezer, saying, 'Thus far the Lord has helped us.'" (Samuel 1 7:12)

Monday — *August 19*

IT was only a small commission, just a minor repair to our favourite garden bench, but when Ron brought it back to us, we saw that he had renovated it beautifully.

"If a job's worth doing, it's worth doing well," he had responded modestly to our compliments, which later set me thinking just how apt that commonplace remark could be. For whether we carry out a task for others or for our own benefit, while there's little satisfaction to be had in doing it poorly, there's no better reward than the pleasure of knowing we've done work to be proud of.

All of this leads me to the conclusion that whoever coined that phrase made a very good job of it!

Tuesday — *August 20*

I'VE got a brand new garden —
I've just moved house, you see,
But, oh, I found my garden
Was empty as can be.
I asked my friends and neighbours
Just what would they advise,
And when I saw their answer
I scarce believed my eyes.
For each had brought a present
A bloom to fill my plot,
From bedding plants to bushes
My friends had brought the lot.
So now my garden's glowing,
Alight with every hue
A quilt of loving kindness
To cheer me all year through.
                    Margaret Ingall

Wednesday — *August 21*

B ORN in 1807 in Massachusetts, John Greenleaf Whittier did not at first seem destined to make much impact in the world. Poor health limited the contribution he was able to make to the struggling family farm, but what he did have was a strong Quaker belief, a gift for poetry and politics and a passionate conviction that slavery was wrong.

To this end he worked tirelessly in every way he could, despite verbal and sometimes even physical attacks from those who opposed such views. This makes it even more remarkable that among his other writings he was able to pen these words of acceptance:

*No longer forward nor behind
I look in hope and fear;
But grateful take the good I find,
The best of now and here.*

A remarkable man of remarkable faith.

Thursday — *August 22*

T HE annual riot of colour in Annie's front garden always brings much pleasure to her neighbours, so when a broken ankle prevented her preparing her usual display of tubs and window boxes, she was delighted when Daphne-next-door offered to help.

"But after I'd filled all the pots with flowers," said Daphne, "I was surprised when Annie asked me to put the best ones immediately under her front windows. When I pointed out that she wouldn't be able to see them from her sofa, she laughed and said it was more important that all the passers-by would!"

I do applaud Annie's unselfishness, so I was more than pleased to hear that her neighbours later clubbed together to buy her a bouquet of her own!

Friday — *August 23*

IMAGINE being a rainbow! Wouldn't that be wonderful? Oh, I know you would look at yourself and see all the shortcomings and the imperfections, then wonder how anyone would ever see you as something that beautiful. Well, take the example of poet Maya Angelou's uncle.

"My Uncle Willie stuttered and had one leg shorter than the other," she wrote. "And yet he was a rainbow in my cloud. I am a rainbow in somebody's cloud. Each of you has that possibility."

So, don't let negative self-image hold you back. Just unwrap your colours and brighten up the sky.

Saturday — *August 24*

EDWARD was more than happy to offer assistance when his neighbour's son needed help with a history project, but was slightly taken aback when young Jake announced that when he was "really old" he hoped he would know everything: "Just like you, Mr Williams."

"I was certainly flattered," Edward said laughing. "But on reflection, I'm very glad that I don't know everything. Just think how boring life would be if there was nothing left to find out about!"

"Experience is never limited, and is never complete," Henry James once wrote.

Sunday — *August 25*

WHAT brings us happiness? I suppose, in today's world, the instant answer is likely to be something along the lines of an exotic holiday or an elaborate piece of jewellery.

Fortunately, we have the Bible to remind us of a far more simple and easily attainable source of happiness. As Proverbs 16:24 reminds us: "Pleasant words are as an honeycomb, sweet to the soul, and health to the bones."

How many pleasant words can we speak today?

Monday — *August 26*

NEIL is a hefty, rugged kind of man. You wouldn't think to compare him to a daffodil or sweet peas! Which is why, when I leaned over his fence to compliment his work, I was surprised to hear him call himself "a gardener and a flower".

Seeing my puzzled expression, he explained: "Some of my plants are useful, some provide sustenance, others might simply brighten someone's day. But they all have a purpose. Each individual flower is special but reaches its full potential only in the company of others. If I could be all those things in God's garden I would be well pleased."

Keep growing, Neil — and keep encouraging the rest of us flowers!

Tuesday — *August 27*

THE importance of mothers has always been recognised in many cultures. According to historians, the ancient Romans held a festival to honour Cybele, mother of the gods.

When we think of mothers, it is also a wonderful opportunity to recognise sisters with children, aunts, mothers-in-law and grandmothers. Here are a couple of memorable quotes to share with the women you love:

"The God to whom little boys say their prayers has a face very like their mothers."   J.M. Barrie

"Youth fades; love droops; the leaves of friendship fall; a mother's secret hope outlives them all."
Oliver Wendell Holmes

Wednesday — *August 28*

REMEMBER not only to say the right thing in the right place, but far more difficult still, to leave unsaid the wrong thing at the tempting moment.
Benjamin Franklin

Thursday — *August 29*

ASKED to think about the words "civilised music" most folk would, I think, imagine a string quartet playing gentle sounds or something similar. But it's perhaps no surprise to hear that the great actor and bon vivant Peter Ustinov had a different interpretation of the term, one which spoke of the joy at the heart of the man while at the same time seeming to so obviously hit the nail on the head.

"The sound of laughter," he wrote, "has always seemed to me the most civilised music in the universe!"

Friday — *August 30*

ON our friend John's writing desk is this goodwill message sent to him by an older friend on his 21st birthday. It still moves him now as much as it did then:

This is to wish you …
Strength for the strife,
Peace for the pathway,
Wisdom for the work,
Friends for the fireside,
Love to the last.

He could not have wished for more inspiring words on that memorable day, ones to cherish for life.

Saturday — *August 31*

FRIENDS sometimes have a way of making us better than we ever think we could be. Describing someone who had an important influence on her, the Nobel Prize-winning novelist Toni Morrison wrote: "The pieces I am, she gathered them. Then she gave them back to me, all in the right order."

Good friends see our lives the way they ought to be – and help us make sure they turn out that way.

September

HERE are anonymous words of reflection to think about today and perhaps you may like to keep them in mind during the week ahead:

May God bless you with discomfort at easy answers and half-truths so that you will live deep within your heart.

May God bless you with anger at injustice and oppression so that you will work for justice, equality and peace.

May God bless you with compassion for those who suffer so that you will reach out to change their pain into joy.

And may God bless you with the foolishness to think you can make a difference in the world so that you will do the things others say cannot be done.

THE world is full of Might-Have-Beens
Or so it feels somehow,
We ponder on the paths we missed,
And never will take now.
But though it's tempting, when we're low,
To think of them and dream,
Such yearning after fantasies
Is foolish in extreme.
For life is Here, and life is Now,
Enjoy what's real and true,
Each life runs just the way it should,
And yours is meant for you!

Margaret Ingall

Tuesday — **September 3**

TWO friends heard about a family where both the mother and one of the children were ill.

"What they need right now is grace," one of them said.

"What they need right now are casseroles," the other one said, and set about making sure the family were fed until the mother was well enough to cook again.

Thankfully, grace comes into our lives in many forms. And sometimes it even disguises itself as casserole dishes!

Wednesday — **September 4**

ONE day I looked up the history of duct tape after seeing a reference to it in a magazine. It was, I discovered, invented for military purposes during the Second World War. It became known as "duct" tape after 1945 when it was used for sealing air-conditioning ducts, although it's apparently not ideal for that purpose.

It is, however, very useful for fixing things around the home if you don't mind the bright silver finish your DIY will have.

Why was I doing this research? Well, because I had just read that in Finland they call duct tape the Jesus Tape. Because, just like Him, it's the saviour of all things broken!

Thursday — **September 5**

JULIE enjoyed her holiday in New York City and had been delighted to find the New Yorkers a helpful, friendly bunch. When she mentioned this to an American friend he responded, perhaps a little cynically: "It's probably because you're a visitor here."

"Well," Julie thought. "Aren't we all?"

Indeed. So let's follow the example the New Yorkers set Julie and be helpful and friendly to everyone else on the same visit.

Time To Unwind

Friday — *September 6*

A YOUNG couple moved into a new neighbourhood. The next morning, while they were eating breakfast, the young woman saw her neighbour hanging up her washing outside.

That laundry was not very clean, she thought — she doesn't know how to do it well. Or perhaps she needs a better washing powder.

Her husband remained silent. Each time her neighbour hung her washing out, the young woman would make the same comment.

One month later, she was surprised to see spotlessly clean clothes on the line and said to her husband: "Look! She has learned how to wash correctly. I wonder who taught her this."

Her husband replied, "I got up early this morning and cleaned our windows!"

And so it is with life: what we see when watching others depends on the purity of the window through which we look. Before we make any criticism, it might be a good idea to ask ourselves if we are ready to see the good rather than looking for faults.

Saturday — *September 7*

L IZ would be first to admit that as a teenager she was too quick to take offence at insensitive words, even when she knew deep down that no harm was intended.

"It took me a little while to realise that the only real enemy I had was myself," she admitted to the Lady of the House.

"Thank goodness I grew wiser. These days I realise that no-one is perfect, including me!"

I think Bernard Meltzer put it best when he reminded us: "When you forgive, you in no way change the past — but you sure do change the future."

Sunday — *September 8*

WHEN Laura agreed to spend her Saturday afternoon being in charge of a stall at the church fête it was with rather mixed feelings, for she had earmarked those few precious hours to repaint her kitchen.

"But I need not have worried," she said later. "Next Saturday afternoon all my friends turned up as a working party and not only did the kitchen get painted, we all had fun doing it."

This brought to mind these words from Luke 6:38: "Give and it will be given to you. A good measure, pressed down, shaken together and running over, will be poured into your lap. For with the measure you use, it will be measured to you."

Monday — *September 9*

HERE are some words of wisdom to help you celebrate your day:

Today is special so use the good cutlery and fancy plates. Don't save them for a special occasion.
No-one is in charge of your happiness but you.
Time heals almost everything. Give time time.
Don't take yourself so seriously. No-one else does.
Believe in miracles.

Tuesday — *September 10*

PROVERBS. We all know a few of these. Some of us are entertained by them, some are educated by them. But what exactly is a proverb? Well, this wry description by Miguel Cervantes, author of "Don Quixote," almost deserves to be one in its own right.

"Proverbs are short sentences," he wrote, "which are drawn from long experience!"

Wednesday — **September 11**

OUR neighbours' daughter Claire has one of the most bubbly personalities of anyone I have ever met. Pupils in several schools where she teaches music love attending her lessons – her enthusiasm is so infectious that it engages even the more reluctant of her young charges.

The Lady of the House commented that getting so much commitment for her choirs and concerts was down to her personality and that she must be blessed with some exceptional qualities.

"I don't know about that," she replied. "My approach to interacting with people is simple and exactly the same that I use to teach music – never be flat, never be sharp, always be natural."

No wonder Claire is such a success!

Thursday — **September 12**

BLUSHING, the sun awakens,
Prepared to welcome day,
Transformed, the trembling moment,
When tired night fades away.

Resplendent, sunrise dazzles,
Painting rose-gold the sky,
Silenced, swift seagulls passing
Like angels flying by.

Awesome in mystic beauty,
Blessing the sleeping scene
Breathtaking, magic moments,
Greet day where night had been.
                  Chrissy Greenslade

Friday — *September 13*

I CAME across these "lessons for life" when leafing through a magazine and they are well worth passing on to you today:

Life isn't fair, but it's still good.
When in doubt, just take the next small step.
Life is too short to waste time being angry with someone.
You don't have to win every argument. Agree to disagree.
Make peace with your past so it won't affect the present.
Take a deep breath. It calms the mind.
When it comes to going after what you love in life, don't take no for an answer.

Saturday — *September 14*

SOME people are under the impression that those who do good only benefit others. But those who actually do good simply smile at the thought, because they know better.

The two-way benefits of helpfulness were neatly summed up by the writer Samuel Johnson when he said: "If you have not often felt the joy of doing a kind act, you have neglected much — and most of all yourself!"

Sunday — *September 15*

IT is said that a minister with a wry sense of humour once prayed for his congregation saying this: "Father, bless us according to our thanklessness ..."

As it dawned on the congregation he might have made a mistake he continued: "Lest Thou bless us according to our thankfulness and we starve!"

With that in mind, let's make sure that if we had to live off our thankfulness we would live a good life: "Now, our God, we give you thanks, and praise your glorious name."

(Chronicles 1 29:13)

Monday — **September 16**

"OLD age doesn't come alone," our old friend Mary's grandmother used to say, meaning it brought a fair collection of aches and pains along with it – but these are external things, nothing to do with the people we really are.

President John Quincy Adams summed up that philosophy well when he wrote: "John Quincy Adams is quite well, but the house in which he lives at present is becoming quite dilapidated. It is tottering upon its foundations.

"Time and the seasons have nearly destroyed it. Its roof is pretty well worn out. Its walls are much shattered, and it trembles with every wind. The old tenement is becoming almost uninhabitable, and I think John Quincy Adams will have to move out of it soon. But he himself is quite well, quite well."

Remember, we are more than our aches and pains.

Tuesday — **September 17**

DO you have a favourite word? One evening, Daphne-next-door had an interesting discussion with a group of friends who offered these memorable examples: serenity, abundance and tranquillity.

All are evocative words surely, but Iris then spoke to say that her choice was serendipity. It's a happy-sounding word coined by Horace Walpole to describe the faculty of making unexpected discoveries by accident. It seems he composed it from the title of a fairy story "The Three Princes of Serendip", an ancient name for Sri Lanka.

Isn't it the small, unexpected things in life which give us so much joy? These little surprises which can brighten a gloomy day. I hope that you will have serendipity in your life to bring a little sunshine when you least expect it.

Wednesday — **September 18**

THE Italian astronomer and mathematician Galileo, who was born in Pisa in 1564, wrote these thought-provoking words many years ago and they are still very much worth thinking about today:

"The sun with all the planets revolving around it and dependent on it can still ripen a bunch of grapes, as if it had nothing else to do in the universe."

Words for us to reflect on with a thankful heart and a sense of wonder at a time of year when the harvest has been safely gathered in once more, the potato crop lifted for the winter and the last of the apples, pears and plums picked.

Thursday — **September 19**

ST Mary's Church in East Raynham in Norfolk stands in the grounds of Raynham Hall, the home of the Townshend family. Rebuilt in 1868 by Viscount Raynham, it was intended that St Mary's would have eight bells, but only three were cast.

However, when at the millennium attention was focused on the ringing of church bells nationwide, it was discovered that the three church bells needed restoration and tuning. This done, the members of St Mary's, with Viscount Raynham as churchwarden, decided that their church should have its eight bells.

A hectic time raising funds to pay for the project followed, and many Townshends scattered worldwide were among those who contributed. Today eight perfectly tuned bells hang in the bell tower and there is a new Ringing Gallery.

Isn't it inspiring to hear what dedication, goodwill and cooperation can achieve? Truly, where there is a will there is a way!

Friday — *September 20*

REV Billy Graham recalled an amusing incident that happened early in his career. He arrived in a small town to preach a sermon. But beforehand he was anxious to post a letter, so asked a young lad in passing where the post office was.

Rev Graham thanked him for the information and said: "If you'll come to the Baptist church this evening, you can hear me telling everyone how to get to Heaven."

"I don't think I'll be there," the boy replied. "You don't even know your way to the post office."

Saturday — *September 21*

EVERY morning Edgar visits his aunt, who lives in a nursing home. Her health is failing and she often doesn't recognise her nephew, but he never misses a day.

When someone asked our friend Stan why he goes to see his wife every day even though she doesn't know who he is, he replied: "She may not know me, but I still know who she is."

Isn't that the kind of love we all want in our lives? It's been said that true love is not physical or romantic, it's an acceptance of all that is, has been, will be and will not be.

Sunday — *September 22*

ARCHBISHOP Desmond Tutu was conducting a service in New Orleans. The congregation might have understood him if he had spoken in English, French or Creole, but they were completely confused when he gave the benediction in Xhosa, a South African language.

Smiling, the archbishop said: "I assure you, He understood!"

And to those unsure how to pray out loud – He understands the unspoken words of your heart as well.

"Then how is it that each of us hears them in our native language?" (Acts 2:8)

Strong Roots

Monday — *September 23*

WHEN Gutzon Borglum's housekeeper visited him at work she was amazed. "How did Mr Borglum know Mr Lincoln was in that rock?" she exclaimed.

Mr Borglum was carving the heads of Presidents of the United States on Mount Rushmore. He knew those faces were in there because he looked at the raw materials with an artist's eye and saw the potential.

Our trials and tribulations are like the little explosions and mighty hammer blows that formed the giant sculpture. A far greater artist than Mr Borglum sees the potential in us and is working ceaselessly to make each of us a monument — a monument to love.

Tuesday — *September 24*

IN 1907, in the slums of Blackburn, a boy was born into the family of an alcoholic stonemason. Money was scarce and although an excellent scholar, the youngster had to leave school aged 13 to spend the rest of his working life in an office. He spent several years studying at night school, gaining qualifications in accountancy.

This man was Alfred Wainwright, author and illustrator of the much-loved guidebooks to the Lakeland Fells. When he discovered the area, he immediately saw it as "magic, a revelation so unexpected that I stood transfixed, unable to believe my eyes . . . I had seen landscapes of rural beauty pictured in the local art gallery, but here was no painted canvas: this was real. This was truth . . ."

Alfred explored the area and captured it in his own distinctive style, inspiring others to discover this magnificent part of the country. His love of beauty has enriched the lives of all those who have followed his footsteps across the Fells.

Wednesday — **September 25**

SO what is the meaning of "life, the universe and everything"? That's the question posed in Douglas Adams' wonderfully comic tale, "The Hitch-hiker's Guide To The Galaxy."

Unfortunately, he reveals, the answer given by the world's greatest computer is "42". The sheer absurdity of such a reply may make us smile, but if we seek a rather more satisfactory answer we might do worse than consider the words of entertainer Sasha Azevedo:

"When you love people and have the desire to make a profound, positive impact upon the world, then will you have accomplished the meaning to live."

I know which I find to be the more sensible judgement.

Thursday — **September 26**

I SEE the sunshine, feel its warmth
I see a sky of blue,
And I rejoice, Lord, once again
And feel so close to you.
Soft breezes stir the plants and trees
There's perfume in the air,
And there is beauty, hope and joy
For You are everywhere.

I see the storm clouds racing in
As winds blow cold and strong,
My problems seem to multiply,
I'm buffeted along.
But life has wonder, love and light
Through all I see and do,
So, Lord, in sunshine or in shade
Please keep me close to You.
Iris Hesselden

Friday — *September 27*

IWONDER if you know the story of playwright and poet Ben Jonson, a contemporary of William Shakespeare? Born in 1573, Ben craved a university education, while his stepfather believed that he should become a bricklayer like him.

Ben soon left to become a mercenary soldier but after a while he returned to England, became a strolling actor and discovered a talent for writing plays.

His elaborate masques were favourite royal entertainment and he became what might be called court poet to James I — Jonson had found his niche in life. By the time he died in 1637 he had become a famous man of letters, the poet who wrote the well-loved lyric "Drink to me only . . ." He is buried in Westminster Abbey.

This true story reminds us that life may present difficulties but with determination we can do our utmost to overcome them.

Saturday — *September 28*

YOUNG Rob will soon be moving hundreds of miles away to attend university. His mother was telling our old friend Mary that it will be difficult for them when Rob leaves home; she and Alan are devoted parents and their family unit is a close one.

But hard as it will be for them to let Rob go, they are confident that the values they have instilled over the years will go with him. They have always encouraged him to work hard and be generous, kind, honest and respectful of others. Alan and June will be filled with sadness when Rob leaves, but they will also be filled with pride and joy to be able to send such a fine young man into the world.

As Ralph Waldo Emerson said: "What we have learned from others becomes our own by reflection."

Sunday — *September 29*

BARNABAS isn't a name that many people recognise from the Bible. However, he sold his field to help support the Apostles and convinced others that Paul was no longer an enemy. He took the side of the insecure young man who would go on to write the book of Mark. Without him, in fact, everything would have been quite different.

Oh, but his name wasn't Barnabas — it was Joseph. Barnabas was his nickname, meaning "son of encouragement" or "the encourager."

Now some folk might aspire to be the centre of attention, but isn't it worthwhile to be less famous and get more done? Try to be an encourager and see what a modern Barnabas can achieve.

"Finally, brothers and sisters, rejoice! Strive for full restoration, encourage one another, be of one mind, live in peace. And the God of love and peace will be with you."

(Corinthians II 13:11)

Monday — *September 30*

OUR friend Rhona uses her computer to chat and share thoughts with family and friends around the world. She recently received an e-mail from a friend in Australia, quoting these lines:

Good friends are like computers,
They "ENTER" your life,
"SAVE" you in their heart,
"FORMAT" your problems,
"SHIFT" you to opportunities,
And, best of all, will never
Press the key marked
"DELETE".

The message in these words, says Rhona, is surely going to appeal to everyone who is familiar with computer keyboards.

October

Tuesday — *October 1*

RECENTLY I heard a story all about kindness in everyday life. Our friend Sylvia had to make a journey one afternoon and because her bus had been a couple of minutes late she had been in danger of missing her connecting train.

When she caught the same bus a week later it was the same driver and he asked if she had made her connection in time.

I believe the passengers on that bus felt all the happier that day for their driver's concern and kindness. Surely it's the same for all of us — we really can make a difference wherever we are, whoever we meet if we make up our minds to do so.

Wednesday — *October 2*

OUR friend Sam finds the words of this prayer inspiring and well worth passing on:
Let me not pray to be sheltered from dangers,
But to be fearless in facing them.
Let me not beg for the stilling of my pain,
But for the heart to conquer it.
Let me not look for allies in life's battlefield,
But to my own strength.
Let me not crave in anxious fear to be saved,
But hope for the patience to win my freedom.
Grant that I may not be a coward,
Feeling your mercy in my success alone;
But let me find the grasp of your hand in my failure.

Thursday — *October 3*

WHO has never experienced that feeling of vulnerability when moving to a new area, beginning a new job, or even joining a club in which there is not one familiar face to be seen? None of us actually likes feeling unsure of ourselves, for security nourishes our roots and gives comfort during the storms of life.

This is why I so admire the courage of people like our friend Paul, who is about to start a teaching post in Nepal, and our old friend Mary's niece Lisa who has just given up a lucrative job to try to make a living as a painter.

Neither are keen to lose the security of the familiar yet both know that, by making an effort to branch out, they may find that their lives will become enriched. The French critic and writer Charles Du Bos put it well when he wrote: "The important thing is this: to be able at any moment to sacrifice what we are for what we could become."

So be brave – even if it is just going out and joining that club!

Friday — *October 4*

THE past can be our teacher
If only we take heed,
And use each bygone error
To be tomorrow's seed,
To plant, this time, with forethought,
Avoiding what went wrong,
To nourish now with wisdom
And help it flourish strong.
Till one day we discover
So bright our seed's display,
It's dimmed our distant sadness
With gladness of today.
                    Margaret Ingall

Saturday — **October 5**

AS a 15-year-old, Amy tended to keep herself to herself and didn't mix a lot with other people. Some thought of her as standoffish, but really she was waiting to know what to do, unsure of herself.

Then, one day, her aunt told her: "You know, Amy, a candle doesn't shine any less brightly for having lit another candle."

It was the reassurance she needed. Since then she has lit up the lives of many others and she herself shines brighter than ever.

Take what light you have and share it. We can all light up the world like that!

Sunday — **October 6**

I WONDER if you have come across this centuries-old prayer by St Ignatius Loyola?

"Dearest Lord, teach me to be generous, teach me to serve you as you deserve, to give and not to count the cost, to fight and not to heed the wounds, to toil and not seek for rest, to labour and not to ask for reward save that of knowing I am doing your will."

Ignatius of Loyola was a Basque nobleman's son, the writer of "Spiritual Exercises" and the founder of the religious order, The Society of Jesus, the Jesuits. Today he is the patron saint of many schools, churches and colleges.

Monday — **October 7**

RECENTLY I heard this wise thought: *The happiest people don't necessarily have the best of everything, they just make the best of everything they have.*

How true!

Changing Seasons

Tuesday — *October 8*

WHO first came up with the idea of clouds having silver linings? Well, in 1634 the poet John Milton referred to a cloud, which should have been dark, that "turned forth her silver lining on the night."

Two hundred years later the novelist Charles Dickens wrote: "I will turn my silver lining outward, like Milton's cloud."

So, we can think of the cloud as a metaphor for difficult situations, but let's not simply wait for them to turn themselves inside out. Because, as Dickens pointed out, the silver lining in those situations can very often be … us!

Wednesday — *October 9*

IF the weather is a little unsettled, or life seems rather mundane, these uplifting words from an Indian statesman are worth keeping in mind: "We live in a wonderful world that is full of beauty, charm and adventure. There is no end to the adventures we can have if only we seek them with our eyes open."

So forget about the weather and the routine daily tasks, just for a moment. Step out into that wonderful world and who knows what adventures you may have?

Thursday — *October 10*

THE 18th-century poet and playwright Johann Schiller once remarked: "When a man is fortunate enough to have several friends, he finds they are all different."

How true these words are, and don't we all know that we wouldn't be without any of our different kinds of friends. They enrich our lives in their own separate ways, just as our various lesser-known passing acquaintances do. Friends come into our lives at many different times and they each add much to the pleasure of everyday living.

Friday – **October 11**

MAIRI runs marathons. She is dedicated to her sport and runs in all kinds of weather. She even runs when she's not feeling one hundred per cent well. Sometimes, some of her friends tell her she is overdoing it and should slow down. One day, she replied, quoting poet T. S. Eliot:

"Only those who will risk going too far can possibly find out how far one can go."

Now that's a challenge to consider. If there's a goal you've given up on, perhaps today is the time to aim for it with a renewed sense of purpose.

Saturday – **October 12**

OUR friend Paula was so pleased to receive a surprise gift of a fridge magnet. The picture on the front depicted a pretty vase of flowers and there were only four words but they said a great deal: *You warm my heart.*

Even more touching was the fact that it had been bought in Canada and brought back across so many miles to Paula's village home. It is now proudly displayed on her fridge door for all to share. How wonderful that something so apparently insignificant can give so much pleasure, surely proof once again that we don't need expensive gifts, just a little kindness and thoughtfulness.

Sunday – **October 13**

MANY faiths have a tradition of judgement at the end of this life, but before we get too despondent, remember there is a saying that goes: "God will one day hold us each accountable for all the things he created for us to enjoy."

Let's make sure that we can say we loved God, loved our neighbour – and had the best possible time doing it!

"Let the trees of the forest sing, let them sing for joy before the Lord, for he comes to judge the earth."

(Chronicles 1 16:33)

147

Monday — *October 14*

WHEN John Capes took over as clergyman of a small but fashionable London church he surprised his flock by asking them to try to bring new faces unfamiliar with the gospels to his services.

He did so himself, sometimes arriving with unexpected kinds of people he had befriended along the way, and some became regular attenders.

He used to say: "Preaching to a church full of believers is fine but to preach to non-believers would be an even greater joy."

Some of his new members were people who had long drifted away from the church. Thanks to him they renewed their faith and found fresh purpose in their lives.

Tuesday — *October 15*

ARGYLL, OCTOBER

OUT at the sea's edge
The whole wind riding the day
The bracken crippled and whipped
The sometimes of light blown away.

Here in huddles of stone
A whole millennium before us
Men from Ireland made chapels
Found God in these blown wide skies.

Further in, where boats nodded and rocked
In little creeks of sun
Under overhangs of oak
We listened to the psalms of blackbirds.
                                        Kenneth Steven

Wednesday — **October 16**

BROWSING through a shop one day, Angela happened to find a collection of the most exquisite paintings. Small and intricately detailed, they depicted children at play during the changing seasons. She bought one each of spring, summer, autumn and winter to hang in her hall.

You can imagine her surprise when she arrived home and discovered who the artist was. Wilbert suffers from cerebral palsy and gets around by motorised scooter. On the back of each painting, he had inscribed a quote by Franklin D. Roosevelt:

Happiness . . . it lies in the joy of achievement, in the thrill of creative effort.

How wonderful to discover that challenges have not succeeded in diminishing Wilbert's unquenchable spirit. His paintings remind us that when life seems overwhelming retreat is not an option.

Thursday — **October 17**

ONE day, the Lady of the House and I were walking along a path by a stream, making our way into town. We had a good-sized shopping list to get through once we arrived, but along the way we shared the delights of a sparkling little waterfall, the sun shining through willow leaves, birds, butterflies and ducks. It was as if nature had dressed up to delight us. There was also a bench halfway along the route.

"It's almost an invitation to sit a while," the Lady of the House remarked.

I reminded her of the list of errands we had to get through before the shops closed. Then she reminded me of the poet Juvenal's words: "Never does nature say one thing and wisdom another."

So, we took the wise option – and sat down for a few minutes to savour our surroundings.

Friday — **October 18**

HAVE you heard of "The Last Brickmaker In America"? It's a film starring the well-known actor Sydney Poitier.

Poitier's character still makes bricks in the old-fashioned way and, to help meet a large order, he takes on a young apprentice. The boy is a troubled teenager whose parents seem too busy to show any interest in him — in fact, they are trying to save their marriage.

Throughout the film the boy, his mother and his father pour out their woes to the brickmaker. He says little in return and rarely offers advice, but because they have someone to talk to each of the characters is eventually able to see beyond their pride and mistakes to the importance of family and love.

Wouldn't it be priceless if we all had someone like that to take our worries to? And if not a brickmaker, then perhaps a carpenter?

Saturday — **October 19**

IT had been a dull and gloomy day but all of a sudden, towards evening, the clouds broke and the sun appeared. In the west, the sky took on a delightful display of colour – sunset that evening was so beautiful!

I thought how that day was so much like our lives. We have times of greyness when nothing much seems to happen. Perhaps we feel life is dull, or even a little boring, but a light suddenly shines out and lifts our spirits. It could be an unexpected visit, letter or a kind word. Something simple but effective and we start to see the sun breaking through the clouds.

May you always find that unexpected ray of sunshine to warm your heart and light up your life.

Sunday — **October 20**

"HOW are you doing?" one man asks. "Oh, I'm feeling great, thanks," his friend replies. Nothing out of the ordinary there, you may think.

Except that in Malawi I believe that they say it a little differently. There the same positive response translates as, "We are doing well, so I'm great!"

It might take a bit of a shift of attitude for our happiness to become dependent on the wellbeing of others, but that is what was meant when, "Sitting down, Jesus called the Twelve and said, 'Anyone who wants to be first must be the very last, and the servant of all.' "

We have it on the best of authority that caring for the happiness of others is the best way to be "great."

Monday — **October 21**

A MAN was watching a butterfly as it emerged from its cocoon. It took so long and was such an agonising struggle for the poor creature that after a while he took pity on it. He found a pair of scissors and gently snipped off the end of the cocoon to set it free.

It emerged but its body was too heavy and its wings too feeble to lift it from the ground. It crawled around for a short time, then died prematurely, never able to fly, never able to feed.

What the man did not realise was that the butterfly's struggle from the cocoon was nature's way of pumping enough fluid into its wings so that they would become strong enough to enable flight immediately.

Sometimes we need to struggle hard to enable us to cope with challenging times. We are presented with these difficulties in order to make us stronger. The greater the obstacle, the greater the achievement.

Tuesday — *October 22*

AS well as being the author of the book "Brave New World" Aldous Huxley, in his later years, was generally considered to be one of the great intellects of his time.

A man like that, who had spent his life studying people and their behaviour, could surely be trusted to come up with some wonderful insight into human nature. It would probably be expressed best, you might think, in the form of a complex philosophy. Not at all — his words are ones we can easily understand.

"It is a little embarrassing," Mr Huxley said, "that, after 45 years of study, the best advice I can give to people is to be a little kinder to each other."

Wednesday — *October 23*

HERE is a gentle prayer sent to me by a reader in Australia and I hope you'll enjoy sharing it:

Blessed is the spot,
and the house,
and the place,
and the city,
and the heart,
and the mountain,
and the refuge,
and the cave,
and the valley,
and the land,
and the sea,
and the island,
and the meadow
where mention of God has been made
and His praise glorified.

Autumn Shades

Thursday — **October 24**

I'VE said it before and I'll say it again — you don't have to be big and important in order to make a difference in this world. Consider the case of Doly Akter.

As a teenager living in one of the poorest areas in Dhaka, Bangladesh, you might think young Doly had every reason to sit back and wait for outside help to come to her. Instead, she made the most of the education that her mother had scrimped to give her by organising her friends into a self-help group offering assistance to the two thousand families who shared their slums.

So successful were Doly's efforts that she was invited by UNICEF to address the United Nations General Assembly.

It's a marvellous example of just how much we can achieve if we are prepared to try. And if one teenager can make such a difference — well, what's stopping us?

Friday — **October 25**

FRIENDS know the song within your heart
And all the dreams you hold,
They know the secrets of your soul
Though they remain untold.

They share your vision for the world
For everyone in need,
They send out caring, healing thoughts
And pray those thoughts succeed.

Friends know the song within your heart
They hope your dreams come true,
Reach out to friends and cherish them
And share their heart-song too.

Iris Hesselden

Saturday — *October 26*

HERE are a couple of quotations which I hope will inspire you to reflect on the pleasures to be found when enjoying the outdoors:

"Climb the mountains and get their good tidings. Nature's peace will flow into you as sunshine flows into trees. The winds will blow their own freshness into you, and the storms their energy, while cares will drop off like autumn leaves."

John Muir

"Keep your love of nature, for that is the true way to understand art more and more."   Vincent van Gogh

Sunday — *October 27*

ACCESS to David's church for people in wheelchairs was over a ramp that had to be taken out and put away each time. After a fortnight's holiday he noticed that the ramp — folded up — was held against the wall, just where it was needed, by a handy little wooden device screwed to the wall.

"Oh, look what Toby did!" he exclaimed, delighted. "Was it Toby?" his wife asked. Then David realised he had no idea who had done the woodwork. But it seemed like the kind of really useful, practical thing Toby would do.

We are known by what we do in this life. Let's live so that when people see good things – they know we did them!

Monday — *October 28*

I CAME across these words by Ovid one day and it occurs to me that they are especially true if we think about holiday journeys made to places near and far: "The use of travelling is to regulate imagination by reality, and instead of thinking how things may be to see them as they are."

Ovid, a Roman writer, composed wonderful tales of ancient days and was both witty and serious. His writing is known to have influenced a number of famous writers, including Shakespeare.

Tuesday — **October 29**

"**W**HO is the person I sometimes see walking your dog?" I asked Sadie.

She explained that he was a younger neighbour who had first offered to walk Muffin, her little spaniel, during a really icy spell. He hadn't wanted her to fall and hurt herself.

"Last winter?" I asked.

"No, three winters ago," she said, smiling. "And once a day every spring, summer and autumn in between!"

Muffin can be quite a determined dog, but not half as determined as some Good Samaritans, it seems!

Wednesday — **October 30**

PEOPLE must have thought Baltasar Gracian, the 17th-century priest and writer, had stumbled upon a miracle cure. Life was a wilderness without it, he wrote. It multiplied blessings, minimised misfortunes, was a unique remedy against adversity and it even soothed the soul.

Now, what could this miraculous "it" be?

I think you may already have guessed, because I'm sure, like Baltasar, you already have at least one of the wondrous items. You see, "it" is a friend!

Thursday — **October 31**

DO you sometimes wake up in the morning and feel that something good is going to happen that day, although you don't know what it will be? Henry Van Dyke described it this way:

For new, and new, and ever new,
The golden bud within the blue;
And every morning seems to say:
There's something happy on the way!

If we can keep that sense of optimism alive in the hours ahead of us, who knows what delightful treasures we may discover?

November

HAPPINESS and joy. You may think that they are very much the same. Joy is a little more exuberant but it's just a difference of degree, surely.

Well, I found another, more important, distinction recently, written by our old friend Anon:

"Happiness depends on happenings. Joy depends on your relationship with life."

WHO were those men, so long ago,
Who caused these stones to stand?
What prompted them to place them here
Upon this rolling land?
Their monuments no secrets tell,
Nor mysteries betray,
And though their feet once trod this grass,
Their world seems far away.
Yet still I cannot help but sense
They too took time to stare
And watch the shadows race the moors,
And breathe the fresh, sweet air.
And though I'll never know their ways
Nor meet them face to face,
I somehow feel their presence near
In this, their special place.

Margaret Ingall

Sunday — **November 3**

NUMEROUS books are written on the subject, academics expound on deep philosophical thoughts, but faith, like most things, is best when it is at its simplest. Or, in this case, its funniest!

"If God says jump through that wall," a good friend once told me, "it's my job to jump – and it's God's job to provide the hole."

"He replied: 'If you have faith as small as a mustard seed, you can say to this mulberry tree, 'Be uprooted and planted in the sea,' and it will obey you." (Luke 17:6)

Monday — **November 4**

LIFE is a learning process. But once we have learned our alphabet and number skills, trained for our chosen career and learned how to balance our budget and run a home, and maybe added another language for pleasure and holiday use, what is there still to learn, you may wonder?

Well, 19th-century Scottish author Henry Drummond, in his book "The Greatest Thing In The World", asked this question: "Is life not full of opportunities for learning love? Every man and woman, every day, has a thousand of them."

So, let's keep learning!

Tuesday — **November 5**

BECAUSE we are guaranteed a new one every 24 hours, the gift of another day can sometimes be taken for granted. But when you think of all the possibilities a day brings it really is a wonder we can sleep through the night. Novelist J. B. Priestley saw it this way:

"I have always been delighted at the prospect of a new day, a fresh try, one more start, with perhaps a bit of magic waiting somewhere behind the morning."

Wednesday — **November 6**

"MY brother is super-fit," Kenneth said. "He visits the gym regularly for a workout which he really enjoys, although annual membership is not exactly cheap. He participates in most of the activities, eats all the right foods and is a supreme example of physical fitness."

"You're not in such a bad shape yourself," I replied. "How do you manage to keep so healthy?"

"Like him," said Kenneth, "I regularly bend, stretch, crouch, reach, stoop, walk, climb, pull, push and eat a well-balanced diet. There is, however, an added dimension to all of this. As a result of my exercise, my family and friends also benefit from my gifts of vitamins, minerals, carbohydrates and fats and proteins."

"How is that?" I asked, looking puzzled.

Kenneth smiled, "Well, you see, I'm a very active vegetable and fruit gardener!"

Thursday — **November 7**

"GREAT oaks from little acorns grow" is a well-used expression, but it was used for the very first time in 1791 when seven-year old Ephraim Farrar took part in his school play. He asked the audience not to expect a performance like the great Greek orators and went on:

"Don't view me with a critic's eye
But pass my imperfections by.
Large streams from little fountains flow,
Tall oaks from little acorns grow."

Those nervously spoken words went on to become a part of our folk-wisdom. So, next time we see someone sincerely trying, but falling short of the highest standards, let's applaud anyway. For who knows what they or their efforts may someday grow into?

Field Day

Friday — **November 8**

THESE lines probably don't qualify as a traditional proverb, and no philosopher seems to have claimed this thought as his own. But today I'd like to share these words for no other reason than, all too often, I have found them to be true and you probably will, too:

"Don't be discouraged," says our fellow traveller. "Remember, it is usually the last key in the bunch that opens the lock."

Saturday — **November 9**

LETTER TO A YOUNG PERSON

THIS comes to wish you great success
In all you can achieve,
A time to step out bravely now,
Be hopeful and believe.

Some others may depend on you
To help them find their way,
But making friends and touching hearts
Will brighten any day.

There may be many hills to climb
With boulders here and there,
But when you reach the mountain top
The future will be clear.

So may the path you choose to take
Hold all you want it to,
And in the years which lie ahead
May life be good to you!

Iris Hesselden

Sunday — *November 10*

DANIEL set out at a brisk pace on a frosty morning. "Right, God," he said to himself. "Another day and thank you for it. Let's see what we can do with it."

Then a thought occurred to him. "Not that you can't do wonderful things without my help. Hope you don't think I'm being presumptuous!"

Just then he slipped on a piece of ice. He'd lost his footing many times that winter and always caught himself in time but this time he went down, landing on both knees.

"Very good, God," he laughed as he knelt there. "Point taken."

"For whoever exalts himself will be humbled and whoever humbles himself will be exalted." (Matthew 23:12)

Monday — *November 11*

IN 1653 the skills of proofreading and editing — even of spelling — were not what they are today. This, then, is why at the end of the introduction to a book published in that year Izaak Walton, the author, begged the reader to, "shew himselfe courteous in mending or passing by some errors in the Printer, which are not so many but that they might be pardoned."

Now, if only we could extend the same courtesy to each other!

Tuesday — *November 12*

FRIENDSHIP is a difficult concept to describe, given that a friend will be different things in different situations. Thomas Burke, who made his name writing about the struggles of the London poor, made a fine attempt at explaining this when he observed:

"True friendship brings sunshine to the shade – and shade to the sunshine."

Wednesday — **November 13**

"A FRIEND in need is a friend indeed." I'm sure we've all heard that old adage, and who wouldn't agree? But to offer your help when it can't actually be requested aloud, or thanked afterwards, is entirely different so I was impressed when I heard about a group called Friends of Friendless Churches.

As their title suggests, this organisation is made up of individuals who, concerned at the number of churches in danger of falling into a state of irreparable disrepair, have decided to "befriend" them. So far they've managed to restore well over 30 attractive and historical buildings, saving them from destruction to become once again an integral part of their community.

I've always believed that the world cannot run without friendship, so it's wonderful to discover a fresh way of expressing it!

Thursday — **November 14**

I CAME across Jake smiling happily as he pulled a loaded wheelbarrow.

"You always seem so cheerful," I remarked, "in spite of your heavy loads."

"That's because it's so much easier to pull a loaded barrow than to push it," he replied. "It's just like life — if I was pushing all my burdens in front of me, friends would soon detect my worries and be concerned. I'd be unloading my problems on them, which is not a happy state of affairs, is it?

"But if I put all my troubles behind me, I can forget them for a while. Out of sight is out of mind. I look and feel happier, and so do my friends."

Let's follow Jake's example and aim to put our cares behind us and push our happiness forward for the benefit of others.

Friday — *November 15*

WE all get it wrong sometimes; say or do something we afterwards regret. The difficult bit is admitting it. I like the way the writer, Alexander Pope, looked at this. He said that if you can admit you were wrong, then you are a better person now than you were yesterday.

Isn't that a thought to reassure?

Saturday — *November 16*

GREAT people don't really need help, do they? Well, designer and patron of the arts John Ruskin had other ideas. "Every great person," he wrote, "is always being helped by everybody."

Well, how does that make them great, then? Mr Ruskin concluded: "For their gift is to get good out of all things and all persons."

In other words if you want to be great, help someone else show what a help they can be.

Sunday — *November 17*

AS the author of the 1930s gardening book "A Fair Beauty" George Sellick must have appreciated the attractions of a well-kept garden. Doubtless he was also familiar with the amount of work involved in keeping a garden beautiful. Looking around at a world many think came about by accident we might ask why it isn't more chaotic; how, indeed, it got to be so beautiful!

"Thus it is," Sellick wrote, "that my small garden leads me to acknowledge the presence of a watching, protecting and ever assiduous Gardener."

"Now the Lord God had planted a garden in the east, in Eden; and there he put the man he had formed."

(Genesis 2:8)

Monday — **November 18**

HAVE you ever heard of "Tubby" Clayton? If not, then you may have heard of Toc H, the organisation he founded during the First World War.

As a serving army chaplain, Philip Clayton knew all too well the stress suffered by soldiers and he decided to create, in a village in Belgium, a rest-house for them. The building was named Talbot House — or in signallers' jargon Toc H — and it was here he created a place of peace for all who needed it, regardless of rank or class.

After the war, many of those who had spent time at Talbot House found it such a valuable experience that they decided to carry on the good work. Nowadays, groups exist all over the world; they are open to all and dedicated to promoting friendship and peace, and to serving their communities in whichever way they can.

Philip Clayton set up Toc H as a beacon of hope in some of the darkest days known to mankind. Isn't it good to know that it's still burning brightly?

Tuesday — **November 19**

THE world's steepest street is Baldwin Street in Dunedin, New Zealand. Rising at an angle of 38 degrees it had to be paved with concrete because tarmac or asphalt would have flowed downhill on hot days.

You would think people would avoid this street. Far from it. Each year competitors race up and down it, several community events are held there and a great deal of money has been raised for charity on its slope. Where some might have looked up the hill and seen a hard slog, others looked and saw opportunities.

Most of the hard slogs in life are like that, so let's try to look on them as Baldwin Streets.

Wednesday — **November 20**

I ONCE heard it said that the more affluent we become, the more complacent we become. Nipun and Guri Mehta would not have agreed with that statement.

Born in the United States and working for an organisation called Charity Focus, they were keen to see for themselves just how the rest of the world lives, so decided to trek through India, living on one dollar a day. Travelling on foot, and with no guarantee of food and shelter, they relied almost entirely on the goodwill of strangers, placing their safety and security, said Guri, "in a kind of trust in the universe".

Was it a worthwhile experience? Yes, for the three-month journey not only strengthened their trust in other people but reinforced their belief that all life should be treated with reverence. Later, they wrote about many of the inspirational people they met.

"I believe in trust and transparency as a spiritual practice," Nipun said. "Trust says you believe, you have faith in the goodness. And transparency says that I'm not going to be overcome by fear."

Not many of us will have the opportunity to walk across India, but this is a lesson we could start to learn much closer to home.

Thursday — **November 21**

HOW can a humble life possibly be of any importance in a world with so many famous high-flyers, you may wonder? Well, the achievers are certainly to be applauded but they are only a part of life, no more or less important than the folk who live quiet lives.

In the Grand Scheme we are all needed and Methodist minister Halford Luccock summed it up beautifully when he said: "No one person can whistle a symphony. It takes a whole orchestra to play it."

Friday — **November 22**

I DON'T know who wrote them but I have always loved these inspiring lines entitled "What I Live For":
For the cause that needs assistance,
The wrong that needs resistance,
For the future in the distance,
And the good that I can do.

Saturday — **November 23**

A BED would seem to be an unusual thing to be proud of. The 18th-century diarist Samuel Pepys was delighted to have such a thing, although not perhaps for the obvious reason.

"Mighty proud I am that I am able to have a spare bed for my friends," he wrote. But I'm guessing he was prouder to have the friends!

Sunday — **November 24**

I WONDER if you know the story of the gentle evening hymn "Glory To Thee, My God This Night" whose last verse is:
Praise God, from whom all blessings flow;
Praise him, all creatures here below;
Praise him above, ye heavenly host;
Praise Father, Son and Holy Ghost.

The writer of these lines was Bishop Thomas Ken (1631-1711), who was appointed Bishop of Bath and Wells by Charles II. He composed this hymn in 1674 for the pupils of Winchester School where he himself had been educated. He also wrote for them the companion morning hymn, "Awake My Soul And With the Sun". Although a quiet and scholarly man, Bishop Ken was fearless in doing what he believed to be right.

Bishop Ken was said to have composed a number of his hymns while making his way along the Rampart Walk at the Bishop's Palace, Wells, in Somerset.

Monday — **November 25**

THERE'S no getting round the fact that it's not been a good time for Hector. Over the past few months his house has been flooded by storm water, a long-anticipated holiday fell through and only weeks later, a fall cost him a broken ankle. Yet throughout, he has continued to face life with resigned good humour.

It was Aristotle who once said: "The beauty of the soul shines out when a man bears with composure one heavy mischance after another, not because he does not feel them, but because he is a man of high and heroic temper."

I'm not sure if Hector himself would claim to have a "high and heroic temper" but I do know that I think he has!

Tuesday — **November 26**

MENTION the name Audrey Hepburn and most of us, I'm sure, will immediately visualise the glamorous star of many favourite films. Fewer will think of her childhood spent in the Nazi-occupied Netherlands, malnourished and fearful — and sadly, perhaps fewer still will remember her in her later years, which she dedicated to being a Goodwill Ambassador for UNICEF.

That time was perhaps the most satisfying of her life. "I have been given the privilege of speaking for children who cannot speak for themselves," she said. "To save a child is a blessing; to save a million is a God-given opportunity."

Audrey Hepburn certainly knew what it was like to feel frightened and helpless, and it's a mark of the strength of her character that even when fame and fortune came her way, she never allowed it to blot out those early memories. Although to many she will be remembered only as an iconic actress, to many more she will be remembered as someone who brought relief and hope into their young lives.

Wednesday — **November 27**

ROGER farms in Yorkshire and many times over the years the Lady of the House and I have enjoyed spectacular views from the top of the hills among the acres of land he tends so lovingly.

"Don't forget that it's grand standing for a while on the hilltops, but the rain washes all the nutrients in the soil downhill, so the best farming is always in the valleys," he told us one day.

He added: "We might think we'd like our lives to be all peaks and no troughs. But when we are in the valley of despair there's no place better for doing some growing!"

Thursday — **November 28**

PRESENT COMPANY

I DO not walk alone
For I am thronged about
With memories, and know
That those who shared awhile
My lifetime's path
Are very near. They flow
Like dappled sunlight
On a constant stream
Throughout my heart and mind
They soothe my soul.
And so, with passing years
I am resigned
To shadows, echoes …
And to music played
In soft, nostalgic tone.
And tho' I may well seem
In solitary state, appearances deceive,
I do not walk alone.
                    Tricia Sturgeon

Friday — *November 29*

DR Robert H. Schuller is the man behind the international Crystal Cathedral Ministries, based in Garden Grove, California. His famous Crystal Cathedral is a massive place of worship constructed of rectangular panes of glass with a congregation of many thousands. Originally, the first services were held in space rented from a drive-in theatre.

Dr Schuller has written more than 30 books and teaches that when our self-esteem is boosted we are better able to find and appreciate the love of God. Take a moment to reflect on some of his uplifting quotes:

"It is difficult to say what is impossible, for the dream of yesterday is the hope of today and the reality of tomorrow."

"If you listen to your fears, you will die never knowing what a great person you might have been."

"I'd rather attempt to do something great and fail than to attempt to do nothing and succeed."

"Today's accomplishments were yesterday's impossibilities."

Saturday — *November 30*

WHEN you are trying to help a friend in need, it's easy to feel that however much you do, it can never be as much as you would like to. Certainly that was how Amy felt when her neighbour Megan was going through a particularly difficult time.

"How I longed to come up with the right words," Amy said ruefully. "But all I could do was just be there." So she was thrilled when later Megan gave her a thank-you card on which she had written a quotation from Margaret Lee Runbeck: "Silence makes the real conversations between friends. Not the saying, but the never needing to say is what counts."

It's comforting to know that sometimes we are of far more help than we think we are.

December

SCOTT has often said that he doesn't have much time for faith. But not long ago he told me about one of the best days of his life. When he was 18 years old he left his rucksack in St Enoch's shopping centre in Glasgow. A man saw it and ran up Buchanan Street to return it to him.

Knowing he must have realised it was empty as soon as he picked it up, Scott asked him why he had bothered. "Because God loves you," the man replied. Then he smiled and walked away. Five years later Scott still remembers how wonderful that felt.

I think that stranger may have delivered more than just a rucksack to my young friend.

"In this way the word of the Lord spread widely and grew in power."   (Acts 19:20)

EVERY time I hear an echo I think of the beautiful maiden who gave us the word. An old Greek legend tells how Echo fell in love with the handsome Narcissus. Alas, he was obsessed with his own reflection and spent every day gazing at it in a pool of water, taking no notice of the lovelorn Echo.

Narcissus became the flower we know today, while Echo wasted away until only her voice was heard, the voice that we hear on the wind.

There is a lesson for us today in this tale. It tells us not to become so wrapped up in ourselves that we neglect those around us, hurting them – and ourselves.

Heading Home

THE FRIENDSHIP BOOK

Tuesday — **December 3**

WHAT can I do? Often people let the fact that they can only do a little prevent them from doing anything at all. To them I offer the true story told in "Acres Of Diamonds" by Rev. Russell H. Conwell.

During the American Depression a young girl was turned away from his church because it was "too busy". Suspecting that her shabby, dirty clothes might have influenced the warden's decision, Rev. Conwell took her in and found her a place.

Two years later, when he took the funeral service of this child of poverty, her mother presented Rev. Conwell with her purse. In it was 57 cents and a note explaining that she'd been saving to help build a bigger church.

This story so touched people's hearts that many thousands of dollars were raised. Today the new Temple Baptist Church in Philadelphia has a seating capacity of 3,300 and a Sunday School building big enough to make sure no child need ever be turned away again.

So don't ask, "What can I do?". Do what you can and God will make of it what He will.

Wednesday — **December 4**

WHAT do you do when you start a new loaf of bread? Throw away the heel? An overseas famine worker has pointed out that we in the West waste the equivalent of millions of precious loaves every year. Now, just think what that could do for starving people.

Since the Lady of the House and I heard this, we have looked at the heels of bread in a different light. After all, they are only slices with crusts down one side. They make delicious slices of toast and scrumptious bread and butter puddings. Try this and see!

Thursday — *December 5*

OUR friend Barry is just back from a once-in-a-lifetime transatlantic trip. He travelled thousands of miles to attend a family wedding and stayed with the groom's family when he arrived.

He discovered that every spare room in the house was accommodating wedding guests and many new friendships sprang up as a result. Later, on the way home Barry read some words by travel writer Tim Cahill that perfectly summed up the experience: "A journey is best measured in friends, rather than miles."

Friday — *December 6*

SOME of us are simply adorable as children. Some are at our most vibrant as teenagers. Coming of age brings new strength and more beauty to more than a few. And some only blossom in later years, once freed from work and family responsibilities.

Actress Jane Fonda thought that when we have our personal springtime is less important than making sure we actually have one. "It doesn't matter if you're a late bloomer," she said. "Just make sure you don't miss the flower show."

Saturday — *December 7*

IT'S a common complaint that we live in a disposable era, where consumer items have built-in obsolescence and few things are worth repairing.

Thankfully we are not, and never will, be in a place where friendships are treated as not worth maintaining, because, as an old proverb states: "None is so rich that they can afford to throw away a friend."

Welcome

Sunday — *December 8*

CAN there be many things more cheering than a chat with a friend? You don't necessarily need to talk about anything in particular but contact with those we know and like still raises the spirits wonderfully.

Now imagine you could take that happy feeling and multiply it. Brother Lawrence, a 17th-century French monk, had something like that in mind when he wrote: "There is not in the world a kind of life more sweet and delightful than that of a continual conversation with God."

"Jacob called the place where God had talked with him Bethel."   (Genesis 35:15)

Monday — *December 9*

IT was a test of horse-power – Canadian style! The Clydesdales were hitched to sledges and weights were added. The winning horse pulled a sledge bearing an impressive 8,000 pounds, while the horse in second place pulled 7,000 pounds.

So, hitched together you would imagine they could move about 15,000 pounds. Actually, it was more than twice that. Together they pulled 33,000 pounds!

Self-reliance is a wonderful thing, but we are capable of so much more with a friend by our side.

Tuesday — *December 10*

THE Fountain of Youth has featured in many a legend, book and film. Of course there is no such thing. Or is there? Actress Sophia Loren had this opinion on the subject:

"There is a fountain of youth," she said. "It is your mind, your talents, the creativity you bring to your life and the lives of the people you love. When you learn to tap this source, you will have truly defeated age."

Wednesday — **December 11**

A SCOTTISH correspondent sent me this beautiful prayer, which has the wonderful story of a saint attached to it:
Be thou a bright flame before me,
Be thou a guiding star above me,
Be thou a smooth path below me,
Be thou a kindly shepherd behind me,
Today — tonight — and forever.

The prayer is that of St Columba, the Irish saint and missionary, who settled with a dozen companions in the year 563 on Iona, off the west coast of Scotland. There, Columba established a monastic settlement of the Celtic Church, and his monks converted the Picts who lived in the north and east to Christianity.

In 597 Columba died on Iona, and during the following centuries, the religious buildings were destroyed. But the island remained a holy place to many, a place of pilgrimage and the burial place of Scottish, Norwegian and Irish kings.

In 1899 ruined Iona Abbey was presented to the Church of Scotland, and it was gradually rebuilt. Then in 1938, inspired by the spirit and faith of the saint, the Iona Community was founded.

Today Iona is both a place of pilgrimage and retreat, an island where St Columba's prayer is echoed by many from all over the world.

Thursday — **December 12**

W E all know people who like to keep themselves to themselves. There's nothing wrong with that, of course, as long as they don't take it too far. There is an old saying: "The more a man gets wrapped up in himself, the colder he is."

We all need the hand of friendship, the warmth that comes with love.

Friday — *December 13*

A WISE person once observed: "The best rule of friendship is to keep your heart a little softer than your head." Just a little softer. Surely even the most stubborn person can manage that. I hope so, because it's generally those of us with the hardest heads who need friendship the most!

Saturday — *December 14*

THE 19th-century Scottish writer George MacDonald said: "A poet is a man who is glad of something, and tries to make others glad of it too."

You don't even have to write anything down, just be glad and share your thoughts. Now, would you like to be a poet today?

Sunday — *December 15*

I WAS just saying goodbye to our friend John when a police car roared by with flashing lights and blaring siren.

"Ah," said John, "time for a siren prayer."

"What do you mean?" I asked.

"Well," he replied, "when you hear the sound of the emergency services it means someone is in trouble. The victim or victims and the rescuers need a spot of assistance and the only help I can bring them is a little prayer for all those involved."

A siren prayer is a splendid idea. Here are some well-chosen words for such an occasion: *Father of love, hear our prayers for the sick members of our community and for all who are in need. Amid mental suffering, stress and anxiety may they find consolation in your healing presence. Show your mercy and free downcast spirits. May these people find peace and lasting health. Amen.*

Monday — *December 16*

SOMEONE wondering how to get ahead in life will find countless books offering all kinds of advice. But a wise man opened his eyes one morning, looked around his bedroom, and found all the advice he needed. Here it is:

The fan said: "Be cool."
The roof said: "Aim high."
The window said: "See the world."
The clock said: "Every minute is precious."
The mirror said: "Reflect before you act."
The calendar said: "Be up-to-date."
The door said: "Push hard for your goals."
And don't forget the carpet, who said: "Kneel down and pray."

Tuesday — *December 17*

CHRISTMAS is on its way again, but did you know that if it wasn't for a certain gentleman named William Winstanley it wouldn't be? He lived some four centuries ago, when the Puritans forbade any kind of celebration; a sad state which lasted for 18 long years.

But when the monarchy returned, Christmas didn't. By then, most people had almost forgotten it was a time for rejoicing — but not William Winstanley. As an established writer, he penned pamphlets, lobbied influential friends and did his utmost to reinstate 25th December as a time of celebration, marking Christ's birthday with carols, dancing and presents, particularly in the form of food and yule logs for the less fortunate, so that they shouldn't be left out of the merrymaking.

Not many people know of William Winstanley, or his campaign, but I do hope I won't be the only one raising my glass to him this year!

Wednesday — **December 18**

AS we all know, words can do many things – they have, for example, the power to heal or hurt, inspire or irritate, delight or distress. So let's resolve to keep these words in mind before we open our mouths:

Know when to speak your mind and when to mind your speech.

Know the difference between keeping your chin up and sticking your neck out.

Thursday — **December 19**

I WONDER if you know the story of the village of Bethlehem in Carmarthenshire, in Wales. How did this Welsh Bethlehem, once named Dyffryn Ceidrich, come to have the same name as the birthplace of Jesus, a name which is derived from the Hebrew *Bet Lehem,* House of Bread?

In 1588 William Morgan, a Welsh Anglican bishop born in Caernarvon, translated the Bible into Welsh, and in doing so he translated the Aramaic name for Christ's birthplace into Bethlehem. Dyffryn Ceidrich's chapel took the name, then in time the village also became known as Bethlehem.

Today many visitors bring or send their Christmas cards to Bethlehem for the village's sub-postmaster to send on their way. There is something particulary appealing about receiving Christmas mail postmarked Bethlehem/Llandeilo.

Friday — **December 20**

THE little girl was captivated by the array of toys on the blanket in front of her. Her grandmother, sitting a few yards away on a park bench, was completely captivated by the little girl.

The smile I am sure she didn't even know she was wearing reminded me of an old and very appropriate saying: "There is something even better than being loved – and that is loving!"

Saturday — *December 21*

IT'S often said that singing or listening to well-known songs is the best way to keep up our spirits when the going gets tough. Here is a ditty by Ella Wheeler Wilcox which has inspired many to stay cheerful during difficult times:

"It's easy enough to be pleasant when life flows by like a song, but the man worthwhile is the one who will smile when everything goes dead wrong!"

Sunday — *December 22*

"HOW many wise men were there?" asked our old friend Mary one day with a twinkle in her eye.

"Three, of course," I replied.

"Multiply that by the number of their gifts," she continued.

"Nine," I said, wondering where this conversation was leading.

"Put the three and nine together . . . 39 — that's the number of books in the Old Testament! Now multiply the three and the nine."

"Twenty-seven."

"And that's the number of books in the New Testament! Add them together and you get the total number of books in the Bible – 66."

Yes, we can try to learn something new every day.

Monday — *December 23*

LEO Tolstoy could write … and write … and write. His novel "War And Peace" was a sweeping epic containing nearly 600 different characters and covering about 1,400 pages. Between its covers the Russian novelist described many profound truths about human nature.

But Tolstoy could be just as profound in many fewer words, such as when he advised: "If you want to be happy – be!"

Tuesday — *December 24*

THERE'S something about Christmas that heightens every feeling — the wonder of the season, the joys of friendship and time spent with those closest to us. But of course, like everything else, it has its reverse side — it can also be when people feel more lonely than at any other time of year. That's why I'd like to share with you this quote from writer Taylor Caldwell, reflecting on the season:

"I am not alone at all, I thought. I was never alone at all. And that of course is the message of Christmas. We are never alone. Not when the night is darkest, the wind coldest, the world seemingly most indifferent. For this is still the time God chooses."

It's a timely reminder that the real everlasting gift of Christmas is the knowledge that we are all — each and every one of us — much-valued members of our Lord's family, from whom we can never be separated.

Wednesday — *December 25*

CHILL breeze,
Leafless trees,
Smoke curls,
Snowflake swirls,
Frosted lawn,
Beds forlorn,
Icy grip,
Haw and hip,
Robins hopping,
People shopping,
Holly hung,
Carols sung,
Bells chime —
Christmas Time!
　　　Brian H. Gent

Thursday — **December 26**

WHEN Abby was young she learned this Christmas prayer in Sunday school written by Robert Louis Stevenson:
Loving Father, help us remember the birth of Jesus
That we may share in the song of angels,
The gladness of the shepherds,
And the worship of the wise men.
Close the door of hate and open
the door of love all over the world.
Let kindness come with every gift
and good desires with every greeting.
Deliver us from evil by the blessing
which Christ brings,
And teach us to be merry with clean hearts.
May the Christmas morning make us happy
to be thy children,
And the Christmas evening bring us to
our beds with grateful thoughts,
Forgiving and forgiven,
For Jesus' sake.
Amen!

Friday — **December 27**

LIKE the Olympic Games the Special Olympics only come around every four years. The challenges overcome during this event are often awe-inspiring and there are lessons to be learned just by watching these sporting heroes.

But the words of the Special Olympics Prayer might just as easily be applied to the difficulties we encounter on ordinary days: "Let me win, but if I cannot win, let me be brave in the attempt."

Now, how could any day not be a gold medal day when faced in that spirit?

Merry Christmas!

Saturday — *December 28*

DILBERT is a cartoon character who appears in over 700 hundred newspapers. When his creator, Scott Adam, first wanted to be a cartoonist he wrote to established television artist Jack Cassady for advice. Jack's reply warned him to expect many rejections on the path to success.

That was indeed what Adam found and soon he put away his inks and gave up. A year later, to Adam's amazement, Cassady, whom he'd never met and hadn't even thanked, wrote again, asking how he was doing. Encouraged again, Adam dug out his inks and Dilbert was created!

Scott Adam believes such kindness can never truly be repaid — and surely it shouldn't be, it should be passed on.

He suggests: "Give your encouragement to someone who can't return the favour — it's a distinction that won't be lost on the recipient. And remember, there's no such thing as a small act of kindness. Every act creates a ripple with no logical end!"

Sunday — *December 29*

ONE afternoon the Lady of the House and I visited a small village church and on the door was this thought-provoking poem:

If after church you wait awhile,
Someone will greet you with a smile,
Though if you quickly rise and flee,
We'll all seem stiff and cold maybe
The one beside you in the pew
Is perhaps, a stranger, too,
All here, we have our fears and cares,
All of us need each others' prayers.
In fellowship we bid you meet
With us, around God's mercy seat.

Monday — *December 30*

WHEN, at the beginning of the 19th century, 28-year-old Miss Maria Hackett chose to take a fatherless boy into her care, her first thought was to give him a good education.

She placed him in the choir school of St Paul's Cathedral, but was soon shocked to discover that little, if any, thought was given to the actual welfare of the boys — and worse still, this was widespread practice everywhere. Young choristers were frequently boarded far from the church, often went without proper meals and spent much of their time wandering the streets alone; their formal education was almost entirely ignored.

Fortunately, Maria Hackett was not one to stand by and do nothing. She began a long campaign to improve matters, and when letters to the clergy were ignored she embarked upon legal action.

At last conditions began to improve, laying the foundations for today's renowned choir schools, in which Maria Hackett is still remembered as "the Choristers' Friend". This gratitude, I'm sure, continues to be sung to the rafters!

Tuesday — *December 31*

HERE are some words which seem to encapsulate to perfection the end-of-the-year days when we are reflecting on life as we stand on the threshold of another year:

Life is a book in volumes three –
The past, the present, and the yet-to-be.
The past is written and laid away,
The present we're writing every day.
And the last and best of volume three
Is locked from sight – God keeps the key.

Photograph Locations and Photographers

FROZEN IN TIME – *View near Cropton, North Yorkshire.*
BUILDING SIGHT – *Kilchurn Castle, Loch Awe, Scotland.*
LOST IN THOUGHT – *Loch Neldricken, Galloway, Scotland.*
DOWN BY THE RIVER – *Ness Bank Gardens, Inverness.*
BEYOND THESE SHORES – *Sanna Beach, Ardnamurchan.*
CAPITAL VISTA – *Looking across Edinburgh from Braid Hills Road.*
SUMMER REFLECTIONS – *St Cado, Brittany.*
HEAVENLY HEIGHTS – *Norwich Cathedral and Maze.*
CLEARLY CLOUDLESS – *Annandale, Dumfries & Galloway.*
WELCOME TO MY GARDEN – *Biblical Garden near Elgin Cathedral.*
CAPTIVATING CORNWALL – *St Mawes, Cornwall.*
TIME TO UNWIND – *Red Point, South Beach, Wester Ross.*
CHANGING SEASONS – *Dalswinton Loch, near Dumfries.*
PRIDE OF PLACE – *On the banks of Loch Ness, Scotland.*
WELCOME! – *Shuswap, British Columbia, Canada.*

ACKNOWLDEGEMENTS: **Marcello Aita:** Beyond These Shores. **David Askham:** Opening Up, Heavenly Heights. **James D. Cameron:** Time To Unwind. **Margaret Ingall:** Field Day. **Douglas Laidlaw:** Breaking Bread, Summer Reflections. **Duncan McEwan:** Welcome To My Garden. **Ian Neilson:** Heading Home. **Chris Nicolson:** Welcome! **Polly Pullar:** Waiting Patiently, Delightful Daffodil, Woodland Wonder. **Phil Seale:** Strong Roots. **South West Images:** Lost In Thought, Clearly Cloudless, Changing Seasons, Autumn Shades. **Sheila Taylor:** Petal Perfection, Where The Heart Is, Fill Your Boots. **thinkstockphotos.com:** Snowgirl, Down On The Beach, Merry Christmas! **Jack Watson:** Down By The River, Pride Of Place. **Richard Watson:** Frozen In Time. **Arch White:** Building Sight, Capital Vista. **Andy Williams:** Captivating Cornwall.